D0680577

344.73   972106   ✓
Strohm, Richard L.
Layman's law guides, Your
 rights in the workplace,

CUMBERLAND COUNTY LIBRARY
800 EAST COMMERCE STREET
BRIDGETON, NJ 08302

WITHDRAWN

DEMCO

YOUR RIGHTS IN THE WORKPLACE

An Employee's Guide To Legal Protection

Richard L. Strohm

CUMBERLAND COUNTY LIBRARY
800 EAST COMMERCE STREET
BRIDGETON, NJ 08302

Chelsea House Publishers

Philadelphia

Copyright © 1994 by Richard L. Strohm

First published in hardback edition in 1997 by Chelsea House Publishers.

1 3 5 7 9 8 6 4 2

Library of Congress Cataloging-in-Publication Data

Strohm, Richard L.
    Layman's Law Guides. Your rights in the Workplace/ by Richard L.
Strohm.
        p. cm.
Rev. ed. of: Your rights in the workplace. 2nd ed. c1994.
Includes index.
    ISBN 0-7910-4442-4 (hc)
    1. Labor laws and legislation—United States—Popular works.
2. Employee rights—United States—Popular works. I. Strohm,
Richard L. Your rights in the workplace. II. Title.
KF3319.6.S77 1997
344.7301—dc21   96-49389
                                                        CIP

972106

This book is published in order to provide accurate information regarding employees' rights. It is sold with the understanding that, while the author is an attorney, the author and the publisher are not engaged in providing legal opinions or other professional services. **Do not** use this book as a substitute for obtaining qualified legal or other professional help.

Instead of writing combinations of the pronouns "he" and "she" as he or she, he/she, s/he, we have elected to use the word "she" uniformly throughout this book when identifying a person. The use of "she" is not meant to be offensive, but is written for the sake of convenience and consistency.

TABLE OF CONTENTS

TABLE OF CONTENTS

TABLE OF CONTENTS

INTRODUCTION

What we do to earn a living is among the most important things in our lives. Employment law, which establishes your rights as an employee, is complicated and confusing. Federal and state legislatures, city halls and town councils have created thousands of laws which affect your work life everyday. Newly created laws are subject to interpretation by the courts, sometimes resulting in expanding or curtailing rights created or implied in the written laws.

There is no one law which covers all employee's rights. Most of the law relating to employment is relatively new and national, or federal. Modern employment law really begins with legislation enacted during or shortly after the Great Depression in the 1930's. Laws relating to discrimination were first passed in the 1960's. Over the years, fine tuning by the federal agencies which administer these laws, as well as courts' interpretations of the laws have clarified employees' rights. The law relating to rights in the workplace is constantly changing, and in a sense, growing.

With so many rules, how can you find out about your rights as an employee? This book was written to help you understand the basic rights you have as an employee, where to get help if you have been treated unfairly, and what kind of benefits and remedies the law gives you as an employee. Knowledge of your rights can provide you with the ability to sort out your options and chart the best course of action.

> *Knowledge of your rights can provide you with the ability to sort out your options and chart the best course of action.*

1

But please remember, this is a small book designed to give you an accurate, but only an overview of employment rights. While the general rules and exceptions are explained, every situation is different. **DO NOT** use this book as a substitute for qualified legal help. Instead, use it as a way of getting solid information in order to understand your legal rights and remedies. The book will be very helpful in learning about your basic rights as an employee or as a tool for preparing for your first meeting with a qualified and skilled employment lawyer, if you decide you need one.

CHAPTER ONE
A WORD ABOUT LAWYERS

Because of the complexity of the various federal, state and local employment laws, I recommend that you first call the specific agency of government involved about any problem or question you have. Each of the federal agencies discussed in this book is there to help you. You do not need a lawyer to file a complaint with any of these agencies. However, a lawyer can be very helpful. Lawyers are helpful in advising you about the "big picture." There may be other solutions to your problem that an agency is not likely to tell you about. In fact, the agency probably will not even know about other rights that you have or damages you may be entitled to collect, but your lawyer will.

Lawyers customarily charge by the hour. Some lawyers do not charge for an initial consultation. To find an attorney, contact your local bar association or lawyer referral service and ask for the name of a licensed, qualified and practicing attorney who specializes in labor or employment law. You may also wish to review your yellow pages under *Attorneys* and *Labor Law*.

A lawyer will help you understand the law and advise you what to do. If you file a lawsuit, he can skillfully guide you through the procedural maze of courts and agencies, making sure to comply with all of the rules and deadlines for filing the various papers required. Lawyers are especially helpful in looking at your side of the dispute and piecing together what the other side's position is likely to

Lawyers are especially helpful in looking at your side of the dispute and piecing together what the other side's position is likely to be.

be. They can then advise you, based on their training and experience, what your chances are of winning in court.

If you do hire a lawyer, remember: A lawyer's first obligation is to you. You are the boss! Even though your lawyer may make certain recommendations, he is working for you, and it is always your decision what to do. Do not do what your lawyer thinks is best if you don't fully understand why you should do it or if you don't believe it is right for you!

You are always entitled to have your calls returned, questions answered, and fees and costs explained. Always obtain a clear written agreement spelling out how your lawyer charges, and how you are expected to pay him. You must trust the lawyer you hire. If, after meeting with an attorney, you feel uncomfortable for any reason, get another lawyer! If you think you cannot afford a lawyer, contact your local community service or legal aid office. You may meet the guidelines for reduced costs or free services of an attorney.

Always obtain a clear written agreement spelling out how your lawyer charges, and how you are expected to pay him.

Some lawyers in private practice will take labor disputes on a *contingency fee* basis. This means that the lawyer will take his fee out of any money that he recovers for you. If he gets no money for you, you have no attorney fee to pay, although *you will have to pay all costs* that he has paid in advance for you.

Customary contingency fees are one third of the total recovery; however, this is subject to negotiation between you and the lawyer. Most lawyers will charge more, say 40%, if the case is more complicated than usual. Some lawyers charge less, if an early settlement can be reached. Whatever agreement you reach with your lawyer, put it in writing!

Remember that even with contingency fees you will be responsible for *costs* which include things like witness fees, filing fees, deposition costs, and expert witness charges. The lawyer may advance these, but he will pay himself back out of your total recovery. If you lose the case and there is no recovery, you will still owe the costs even though you do not have to pay the lawyer's fee for the time he has spent on the case.

If you lose the case and there is no recovery, you still owe the costs even though you do not have to pay the lawyer's fee.

The costs in a suit can be very high, particularly if your lawyer thinks you need to hire professional or expert witnesses. Make sure you get an estimate from the lawyer on costs, and make sure you put in writing that the lawyer will not hire experts without first getting your approval.

If you feel your lawyer is not representing you well and you lack confidence in him after you have explained your concerns and tried to work it out with him, you are not obligated to continue to use his services, even if you have signed a fee agreement. You may fire him and obtain new counsel. However, you may still owe him for time he spent on your case before you relieved him. He may also be entitled to a lien on your recovery to the extent of the time he has spent on your case.

But be careful! Before you fire your lawyer, first make sure another lawyer will take your case on terms agreeable to you. Make sure that you do not wait too long. The longer you wait, the less likely it is that a new lawyer will take your case even if you have a good claim.

When selecting a lawyer, ask:

- How is the fee computed and what expenses will I be billed for?

- Who, besides the lawyer, will work on the case and what will their fee arrangements be?

- What experience does this lawyer, not the firm, have with this kind of case?

- Has he gotten results in previous, similar cases?

- How long has this lawyer been practicing?

- What kinds of cases does he usually handle?

- How much will fees and costs be per month until the case is resolved?

- How much, approximately, will the case cost to process altogether?

- How long will the case take to process?

It is reasonable to request written monthly status letters explaining the progress of your case.

It is a good idea to require the lawyer to send you monthly statements describing all time he and others in the office have spent on your case, and itemizing all of the costs he has paid or incurred. It is also reasonable to request written monthly status letters explaining the progress of your case or claim. You should also request and receive copies of all documents received or sent by your lawyer concerning your case.

CHAPTER TWO
FEDERAL LAWS AND
ADMINISTRATIVE AGENCIES
. . . .

Before we discuss what rights you have as an employee, you need to have an understanding of the source of your rights. As Americans, we enjoy a *federal* system, meaning that the federal law is supreme. Federal legislation is the source of most employment related rights. Whatever has not been already regulated by the federal government can be regulated by the state legislatures. The state legislatures are free to expand the rights given to every American citizen by the federal system, so long as the laws of the state do not conflict with the laws of the federal government or the United States Constitution. In other words, no state can enact a law which takes away rights which have been created by the federal government.

> *No state can enact a law which takes away rights which have been created by the federal government.*

Under this federal system, however, the law of sister states may be very different. In fact, state laws often conflict with one another without conflicting with federal law. This creates a very troubling problem, particularly if you are being advised by someone who lives or has experience in another state.

The bottom line is this: all Americans who are employees enjoy certain protections established by the United States Constitution and federal law. There may be additional rights in some states which are not found in others. Employment law is a creature of *statute*, that is, written law. The written law is then interpreted and refined by judges in court decisions.

Employment law is further complicated because the United States Congress has created *agencies* to administer employment laws. For example, the Americans With Disabilities Act (ADA) was created by the United States Congress in late 1990, effective July 26, 1992. An existing federal agency called the Equal Employment Opportunity Commission (EEOC), administers this law.

How is an employment related law *administered*? An administrative agency is created by Congress and empowered to do that which is necessary to carry out the intent of Congress in creating the law. So in my example of the ADA, the Equal Employment Opportunity Commission (EEOC) enacts and enforces rules which are just as important as the actual law created by Congress. The agency's rules of procedure are very important.

In addition to creating rules and regulations, the agency charged with enforcing an employment statute usually conducts investigations and hearings and makes decisions about whether the law has been violated. The various administrative agencies are there to help you. There are local offices of federal agencies; just look them up in the blue pages in the telephone book. You always have the right to file a complaint directly with an agency.

If you feel your rights have been violated, the first step is to contact the agency which oversees the law and fill out a complaint.

If you feel your rights have been violated, the first step is to contact the agency which oversees the law and fill out a complaint. They will help you. The agency will then investigate and make recommendations, if there has been a violation, which your employer must obey. In the event your employer does not comply with an agency recommendation, the matter can be referred to the United States Department of Justice for legal action. Some of the employment laws have criminal as well as civil penalties for violation of an employee's rights. This means that in addition to the agency ordering an employer to change its procedures and perhaps rehire an employee, an employer could be criminally prosecuted and sent to jail for violating the employee's rights (If the employer is a corporation, a managing agent would serve the time).

An employer could be criminally prosecuted and sent to jail for violating the employee's rights.

The states often have laws similar to those of the federal government. Sometimes a state agency investigates complaints in an area where both the state and federal authorities have similar laws. In these circumstances, there may be an agreement between state and federal authorities regarding which agency, state or federal, will investigate certain types of employer conduct. So it is also important to call the agency before you file any complaint.

The various federal laws which are discussed in this book are *cited*. That is, the official name and location of the statute is given so that you can review, on your own if you choose, the exact law I am discussing at your local library. Now lets take a look at your rights as an employee!

CHAPTER THREE
WHAT BASIC RIGHTS DO I HAVE AS AN EMPLOYEE?
· ·

What Is an Employee?

What rights you have in the workplace depend primarily on whether you are an *employee*. If you are not an employee, then rights of the workplace do not apply to you.

Generally an employee is someone who (1) works for someone else, (2) works for pay and (3) is *controlled* by the person who pays him. *Control* is a legal term meaning that the employer determines the type of job the employee does and the method in which he does it.

Independent Contractors Are Not Employees

> *An independent contractor is someone who is independent of control by an employer.*

By contrast, an independent contractor is someone who is independent of *control* by an employer. Generally an independent contractor is someone who performs a service for (1) another, (2) for a fee and (3) in a manner entirely up to the independent contractor and the person or entity for whom the service is performed. For example, an independent contractor has an agreement with a local bank to clean the bank after the workday ends at 5:00 p.m. The contractor may come in at 6:00 p.m., 7:00 p.m., 10:00 p.m. or 3:00 a.m.! He stays eight hours or 15 minutes, however long it takes him to complete the job he has contracted to do. The bank manager does not tell him how to clean, what equipment to use, how many people he should use to staff the job, or what kind of cleaning products to use. The independent contractor has been hired (by means of a written or oral agreement) to do a particular job, and how the job is done is entirely up to the independent contractor.

An employee, however, is required to start and finish the workday at a certain time. His work must be performed in a manner outlined by the employer, and performed at a certain place and in a certain way, usually using tools and materials supplied by the employer. An independent contractor negotiates a price for the job he does and gets paid if he does the job properly. An employee earns income based on the period of time he works for his employer.

Because the independent contractor is not an employee, he is not given any employment benefits, such as health, life, dental insurance or workmen's compensation. There is no time-and-a-half, sick leave, or vacation time. Although independent contractors may be used over and over to do certain jobs, they are not supervised by the person hiring them, and they provide their services purely on a contract basis. Independent contractors do not get W-2s, and the Internal Revenue Service does not consider them to be employees. Instead of a W-2 form, they receive a form called a 1099, showing *miscellaneous income*, as opposed to the W-2, which shows wages, tips, or other income paid by an employer.

Because the independent contractor is not an employee, he is not given any employment benefits.

Independent contractors are not employees, and therefore all the rights of the workplace which apply to employees, do not apply to them. If you are an independent contractor this book won't help you much. Any problem you have must be resolved by the terms of your contract, usually through arbitration or the courts. But if you are not an independent contractor, read on!

CHAPTER FOUR
THE RIGHT TO BE PAID
•••

The primary right of an employee is to be paid for the work done and time put in on behalf of the employer. While this appears to be obvious, there was no law imposing penalties against employers who reneged on meeting payroll until the twentieth century!

> *The primary right of an employee is to be paid for the work done on behalf of the employer.*

During the Great Depression in the 1930's, labor strife was rampant in America. As a result of the lack of jobs and the inability of workers to fairly and adequately bargain with their employers, Congress enacted the Fair Labor Standards Act (FLSA) in 1938. Its purpose was and is to regulate wages and hours of those workers who were producing goods for commerce. If you are interested in studying this act, go to your public library and ask to see the United States Code. The act is found in Volume 29 of the United States Code at Section 201. The *cite* is 29 U.S.C. Section 201.

The United States Department of Labor (USDL) is the administrative agency which creates rules concerning the implementation of the FLSA, and brings lawsuits against employers who fail to pay minimum wage or overtime compensation. The Wage and Hour Division of the United States Department of Labor (USDL) specifically manages complaints arising under FLSA.

FLSA allows an employee the right to recover money damages in the event an employee proves his employer violated this Act. The government will usually not initiate a lawsuit on behalf of a single employee. If there are a number of employees affected by the unlawful practice of a particular employer, then the U.S. Department of Justice is likely to get involved. I recommend that you first file a complaint with the Wage and Hour Division of USDL, obtain your wrongfully withheld wages and then hire a private lawyer to begin a lawsuit for additional damages, if any. Get a lawyer to help you.

FLSA also sets minimum wage and overtime pay requirements. However, there are a number of exceptions to this law, which include:

- Farmers or others, including children engaged in agriculture

- Small retail and service establishments whose total sales measured in gross annual receipts are less than $250,000

- Professional employees and executives

- Severely physically handicapped persons

- Trainees

- A variety of persons who work at home

- Domestic workers who earn less than $50 per quarter from any employer

- Waiters, waitresses, bartenders

- Non-resident employees

- Truckers, cab drivers and some common carrier drivers

If you are unsure whether you are in an exempt category, call your local office of the United States Department of Labor. The num-

If there are a number of employees affected, then the Department of Justice is likely to get involved.

ber can be found in the blue pages of the telephone directory under United States Government—Department of Labor.

The Minimum Wage

The minimum wage is now $4.25 per hour, effective April 4, 1991. Each state may have a higher minimum wage, but no employer can pay a lower wage. In addition, the Davis/Bacon Act, 40 U.S.C. Section 276, provides that any worker who performs services or labor pursuant to a contract with the federal government must receive the *prevailing wage* rate for the type of work that is being performed in that location.

Compensatory Time

FLSA also requires that an employer pay an employee at one and one-half times the *regular rate* for hours worked in excess of 40 hours per week, which is defined as seven consecutive days. The law permits the employer to change the work week cycle if the change is expected to be permanent. In other words, the employer cannot simply change around the work week to avoid having to pay the employee.

The employer cannot simply change around the work week to avoid having to pay the employee.

The law also says that the employer must pay the overtime in a timely manner. Please keep in mind that there are a number of exceptions to the maximum hours provisions. Hospitals, nursing homes, and other medical centers are allowed to use a different formula which may be based upon 80 hours in a 14-day period.

FLSA also generally prohibits private employers paying workers through the use of compensatory time off (*comp time*) for overtime work.

However, employees of state and local governments may be given compensatory time off instead of overtime pay. To be sure, call your local office of the U.S. Department of Labor.

Child Labor

Because working children before 1938 were often neglected, cruelly overworked or subject to unduly harsh conditions, a provision within FLSA was enacted to correct these abuses. The law states that one must be at least 14 years of age to work in a non-manufacturing or similar *non-hazardous* job, provided that 14 year-olds who are so employed are limited to part-time work only (or 18 hours per school week and only three hours for each school day). Other restrictions also apply.

In order to work full-time, a child must be 16, or 18 to work in an occupation which the Department of Labor considers hazardous.

In order to work full-time, a child must be 16, or 18 to work in an occupation which the Department of Labor considers hazardous. These rules do not apply to farm children (who are protected by the more relaxed rules found in the Agricultural Workers Protection Act, which also covers migrant workers) or to child actors, paper boys, etc.

For more information write:

Child Labor Programs
Employment Standards Administration
Department of Labor
200 Constitution Ave., NW, Room S-3510
(202) 523-7640

Migrant Workers

The Migrant Agricultural Workers Protection Act, in addition to protecting children, gives rights to migrant farm laborers. This law requires that the employer disclose in writing (1) wages to be paid, (2) where the worker is to work, (3) the terms of employment, (4) a list of the employee benefits and (5) pay deductions charged to cover those benefits. This law also requires employers to give each worker, with his pay check, a complete breakdown of how his pay was computed including the hours worked, compensation rate, and detailed explanation of all pay deductions.

The Company Store and Company Deductions

Under the FLSA, an employer generally cannot deduct the value of tools of the trade or the cost of uniforms from your pay. Nor can he take deductions from your pay which have not been disclosed to you before you started working for the employer.

An employer generally cannot deduct the value of tools of the trade or the cost of uniforms from your pay.

The company can, however, deduct for damage to the employer's materials or other property which you caused, but only on earnings above the minimum wage. So if you earned only the minimum wage, the employer could not take anything out of your pay check even if you broke something belonging to the employer.

What Else Can I Do if My FLSA Rights Are Violated?

If your rights have been violated, your first recourse is to the Department of Labor. To file a complaint, first obtain the appropriate forms from your local office of the Department of Labor. A sample complaint form is shown on page 1 of the Appendix. Either you or the Department of Labor staff will prepare the form. The department will then conduct an investigation. Your identity can be kept confidential. If the Department of Labor finds violations, it will attempt to settle the matter with your employer. This agency can order the employer to pay your back wages, and if the employer fails to comply, it can file a lawsuit seeking back wages and a court order preventing the employer from continuing the unlawful practice.

You can also sue your employer on your own for back wages plus your attorney's fees and costs. Contact competent counsel if you are considering a lawsuit. In no circumstance should you be intimidated from filing a complaint because you fear retaliation or the loss of your job. The law provides civil and possible *criminal* penalties to any employer who fires or mistreats an employee because he has filed a FLSA complaint, even if the complaint is later to be determined to have no merit by the Department of Labor.

In no circumstance should you be intimidated from filing a complaint because you fear retaliation.

What If I Am Not Paid All That I Am Owed?

If you are not paid what you are owed and your employer refuses to pay for hours worked or commissions earned, you may have additional rights under your state's laws. Not being paid minimum wages or overtime pay which you have earned is clearly a violation of FLSA, and you should file a complaint with the Department of Labor and recover your back wages. You are also entitled to sue your employer.

Most states allow a wronged employee to recover additional damages, sometimes two or three times the amount the employer owes in addition to attorney's fees, costs and other damages for a failure to pay wages. This is to deter employers from not paying its employees' earned wages. Again, this is an area where you need professional help. Remember that the federal agency will not be able to help you prosecute your claims in state court. In other words, USDL can help you get your back wages but it cannot help you get double or triple damages which your state law allows. You need a lawyer's help for this.

Remember, the federal agency will not be able to help you prosecute your claims in state court.

CHAPTER FIVE
THE RIGHT TO BE EMPLOYED: WHEN CAN THE BOSS FIRE ME?

Contract vs. *At Will* Employees

Since employment is a creature of contract, that is, working for an employer is a matter of an agreement between the employer and the employee, whatever the parties negotiate and agree upon is the starting point for determining when the boss can demote, discipline or terminate you.

You may have a written agreement which sets up the terms of the employment, or you may have an oral agreement, that is, an agreement based on a conversation or series of conversations with your employer. Or, you may have started working based on unstated assumptions that both you and your employer had about the job.

All employment relationships are considered by the law to be contractual, even without any written agreement.

It is always best to have a written agreement, but usually this is not always possible. However, all employment relationships are considered by the law to be contractual, even if you are simply put on the payroll without any written agreement about pay or job duties. If you have no written contract with your employer which specifies how long you are to be employed or when you may be demoted or terminated, you are considered to be an employee "*at will*," because *you may be fired at the will of the employer.*

The history of employment law, until very recently, has been that employers had almost unlimited discretion in hiring, promoting, and firing whomever they chose, and for whatever reason they saw fit. Today, employers still have a great deal of discretion, but their actions are subject to 1) the terms of any contract they have with their employees; 2) the federal and state employment statutes; and 3) public policy.

In determining your rights as an employee, you must first look to all of the documentation surrounding your relationship with your employer. This includes letters, bulletin board notices, training manuals, procedural manuals, any *writing* which concerns you individually or all employees in general. These documents are sometimes interpreted by the courts as part of the employment contract between you and your employer. These documents may create or imply rights for you that you had no idea you had!

In determining your rights, you must first look to all the documentation surrounding your relationship with your employer.

For example, assume that you have no written contract with your employer. However, your company has an employment manual which states that no one will be fired without *just cause*. Then you are fired simply because the boss wants to make room for a relative. Normally, without a written contract with your employer containing a specific provision forbidding such action, the employer could legally terminate you to make room for his incompetent nephew, because you are without an employment contract and merely an *at will* employee. But because of the *just cause* provision in the manual, a court is likely to hold that this is a promise made by the employer to all its employees, even though implied *at will*. And since being terminated because of the boss's callous need to find work for his n'er-do-well nephew does not constitute *just cause* to fire you, you would probably be entitled to your job back with back pay. This is because the employer breached its promise made in the manual to all employees, including you, not to fire anyone without *just cause*.

In other words, the employer's termination of you is in violation of your contractual rights. So you can see that the written materials of the company are very important because they may create contract rights for you. You then have the right to enforce these rights against the employer in the event he refuses to honor them.

The written materials of the company are very important because they may create contract rights for you.

Please note that you may be required to arbitrate any dispute with your employer if your employer's policies provide for arbitration of employment disputes. This means that you cannot sue in court but that you must follow the arbitration procedure set forth in the employer's policy.

You also need to check to see if there is a *disclaimer* in the employee manual advising you that the booklet is for informational use only and does not constitute any promise to the employee. We'll discuss disclaimers a little later, on page 24.

By the way, a *just cause* provision like the one in our example is very unusual. Employers or their attorneys usually are very careful in crafting employment manual statements so as to avoid the very result in the example. So, if you want protection from firing without *just cause*, negotiate this point and put it in writing. It doesn't have to be fancy—a letter signed by your employer will do or even a letter from you to your employer acknowledging that "...you have agreed that I will not be terminated except for just causes..." is better than nothing. Negotiate with your employer, get the terms of the agreement hammered out, put it in writing and get the employer to acknowledge or sign it!

Wrongful Termination

In most situations, employment is without a contract and therefore *at will*. Employers are very reluctant to create rights which may cause them problems later on. Generally, an employer may fire you at anytime, for any reason, if you have no contract saying otherwise. I said *generally* because there are many exceptions, such as employment discrimination, which I will discuss in a moment. *At will employment* means that an employer can terminate an employee hired for an indefinite period of time for good cause or for no cause at all. Likewise, an employee is free to quit for whatever reason he wishes.

In the 1980's, the concept of *employment at will* saw two major exceptions created by the courts: (1) implied contract or agreement, and (2) public policy.

Implied Contract

As with my example of the employee manual, an implied contract or agreement is based upon the statements or conduct of an employer. Employers have frequently been required to honor terms of employment contained in policy statements, employee handbooks, or manuals which the employee has received. In other words, what is contained in your employee handbook, posted notices, interoffice memos on company policy,

Generally, an employer may fire you at anytime, for any reason, if you nave no contract saying otherwise.

can be considered a set of promises made by your employer to you.

Employee disciplinary procedures, including language such as *cause* or *just cause* in the employment manual, may also suggest that employment *at will* was not intended. If there is a probationary period provided, some courts have indicated that employment is permanent once the probation period is satisfied. In this interpretation, the employer may not fire you for any reason except good cause.

Disclaimers and Just Causes

A *disclaimer* is a denial by the employer that he is conveying employment rights to you. Employers obviously want to do as little as possible—usually only what the law or marketplace minimally requires.

However, employer conduct, comments or other employer documents, which conflict with disclaimers, may erode the effectiveness of the disclaimer. Keep in mind that although clearly it is better to have a promise in writing, oral promises in the employment context have been enforced by the courts. In one case, for example, an employee asked his supervisor about the company's policy on job security. In response, he was told that as long as his performance was satisfactory he would not need to worry about termination. The court found a *just cause agreement* created by this exchange of comments between employer and employee. But remember, oral promises may be difficult to prove. Its your word against the employer's—and you, not your employer, has the burden of proof! The legal term, *just cause,* defies easy definition. Its

Although clearly it is better to have a promise in writing, oral promises have been enforced by the courts.

meaning depends upon the facts of each case and the nature of the employer's industry or business. One court has defined *just cause* to mean "a fair and honest cause or reason, regulated by good faith on the part of the party exercising the power."

Although this view of just cause is not held by all courts in all states, it does give the term enough meaning to make the idea understandable. The point is that if you negotiate a *just cause* provision in your employment contract, or the courts find one from your employers contract or writing, you are protected from being fired at the whim of the employer.

Public Policy

An employee may also by protected by the courts from being fired at will, if he has been terminated for reasons which violate *public policy*. Even if you are an employee *at will* you cannot be fired if the firing violates the laws or public policy of the state or federal government. The classic example is race discrimination. A black *at will* employee cannot be fired one day simply because he is black.

Even an employee "at will" cannot be fired if it violates the laws or public policy.

Courts in some states have found that employees who are discriminated against in violation of anti-discrimination laws, may also sue in court for *wrongful discharge* because anti-discrimination laws form a part of the state's *public policy*. This is very important! An employee allegedly terminated for reasons of national origin may have two possibilities for relief: He may have 1) a case under the Equal Employment Opportunity Law which is brought before the federal, state or local equal employment opportunity agency (I discuss this on page 30) and 2) a suit for money damages based on wrongful discharge for violation of the state's public policy, which would be brought in the court system.

Although there may be two routes for relief, the remedies for each of these paths is distinct. If you win at the agency level, you get your job back. But if you win in state court, you get money damages for your loss as well as punitive damages if the employer's conduct is reckless or intentional. Punitive damages, which can be considerable, are a potential for a claim for wrongful discharge based on *public policy*.

Your state's constitution, statutes and judicial decisions in addition to the federal laws comprise what is considered *public policy*. Each state is a little different, so contact an attorney if you have been fired. Besides discrimination, some typical examples of lawsuits based on public policy grounds entitling the employee to collect money damages include:

- employees who are terminated for jury service or filing workmen's compensation claims;

Part of the public policy doctrine includes claims made by so called "whistle blowers."

- employees who refuse to commit perjury;

- employees who decline to engage in price fixing;

- employees who report illegal activities of their employers.

Part of the *public policy* doctrine includes claims made by so-called *whistle blowers*. Check your state law because it may have its own whistle blowing statute prescribing additional rights.

For more information on your rights concerning the reporting of fraud, abuse or waste within the federal government, or to report such fraud, abuse or waste, contact:

Inspector General's Office,
Department of Commerce
14th Street and Constitution Ave., NW
Room 7898C
Washington, DC 20230
(800) 424-5197
(202) 377-2495

CHAPTER SIX
WHAT LAWS PROHIBIT DISCRIMINATION IN THE WORKPLACE?

The general rule is that an employee can be fired for any reason, at any time, unless there is a contract (in writing or implied) which says otherwise, or if the employer's action violates public policy. What is a violation of public policy in the context of federal employment law? At a minimum it is discrimination based on race, color, religion, sex, national origin, age and disability. There are a number of federal laws which prohibit employment discrimination based on these factors.

Title VII, The Civil Rights Amendment

The first and most comprehensive law prohibiting discrimination in the workplace is called *Title VII* of the Civil Rights Act of 1964, as amended. Find it at 42 U.S.C. Section 2000(e). It was enacted to prevent employers from discriminating against an employee or applicant for employment on the basis of race, color, religion, sex (including pregnancy) or national origin. The law applies to all state and local governments and educational institutions, employment agencies, labor unions, and all private employers with 15 or more employees.

Title VII prevents the employer from discriminating on the basis of race, color, religion, sex or national origin.

Title VII essentially lists a number of *unlawful employment practices* and prevents the employer from discriminating in advertising for jobs, hiring, firing, terms and conditions of employment, including compensation and fringe benefits, as well as opportunities for advancement. It is also illegal for an employer to retaliate against an individual because he has made a claim or tried to enforce his rights under this part of the law.

As in all things with law, there are some exceptions. Title VII does not apply to Indian tribes or private memberships (which are tax exempt under 501(c) of the Internal Code). Employment agencies are specifically covered, as are labor unions provided they have a hiring hall or have 15 or more members. State agencies or other government entities are not exempt from coverage and must comply like every other employer.

The Act describes what employment practices *do not* violate the law. They include:

Treating employees differently when the different treatment is required by the job. (For example, an employment position where the sex of the individual is important to the job. A modeling agency in the business of providing models for women's clothing would require a woman to fill employment slots and would be held to be a "bona fide, occupational qualification");

A policy by a religious supported educational institution to employ only those who have the same sort of religious beliefs as the religious groups supporting the institution;

Where the individual is a communist party member;

When the discrimination is based on seniority, merit or other bonus system which is specifically not reflective of an intention to

It is illegal for an employer to retaliate against an individual because he has made a claim under Title VII.

discriminate because of race, color, religion, sex or national origin;

Firing an employee when the individual is a threat to national security or when that individual lacks the background sufficient for security clearance.

Filing a Title VII Claim

If you think that you have been the subject of discrimination based on account of race, color, sex, religion, or national origin, file a complaint with the nearest office of the United States Equal Employment Opportunity Commission (EEOC). Please remember that employment discrimination complaints must be filed with the EEOC within a very short time of the discrimination, usually within 180 days.

Employment discrimination complaints must be filed within a very short time of the discrimination.

In some states where there is a local state office which reviews discrimination complaints, you may be required to file with the state rather than with the federal office. Call the EEOC toll-free at (800) 872-3362 to find out whether you file with the state agency or with the local federal agency. When you call, ask for information about the deadline for filing and where the complaint must be filed.

While you have the right to sue in the courts (in addition to filing a complaint with EEOC) you may not sue your employer in court for damages for discrimination without first filing an EEOC complaint! This is very important. **THE LAW ALLOWS DISCRIMINATION SUITS AGAINST EMPLOYERS BUT ONLY AFTER YOU FIRST FILE A COMPLAINT WITH THE EEOC.** If you wait too long (longer than 180 days from the date of discrimination, generally) or if you fail to first file with EEOC and the statute of limitations runs out, you will probably lose your right to sue your employer in court for discrimination, even if your claim is a good one.

The EEOC has a toll free hotline which is designed to allow you an opportunity to report discrimination directly. There is also an opportunity, when using this line, to confer with a government lawyer to obtain guidance about your particular set of circumstances. Contact:

Equal Employment Opportunity
Commission
1801 L Street, NW
Washington, DC 20507
(800) USA-EEOC

Investigation of Title VII Claims

After you file your complaint with the EEOC or appropriate local agency, you will be interviewed about the facts by a government worker. The government notifies the employer of your claim and requests pertinent information from them. Any witnesses having knowledge of the facts will be interviewed. The employer should cooperate; but there is no guarantee. The government may subpoena the production of important documentation. The employer may offer settlement without further activity; the government generally encourages settlement.

After you file your complaint, you will be interviewed by a government worker.

The government investigates your claim and tries to figure out if your claim is valid. If you are able to show that your claim of discrimination is arguably meritorious, it then becomes the burden of the employer to show that there is some

31

other difference between employees that justifies different treatment. The key here is exploring all of the possible differences between the employees. If the employer shows that there is good reason for the different treatment, then there can be no finding of discrimination. This is called the *disparate treatment* theory of discrimination.

If the employer shows there is good reason for the different treatment, there can be no finding of discrimination.

Another theory, called *the disparate impact* theory, holds that an employer's hiring practices, although appearing neutral and unbiased on the surface, tend to disfavor members of a certain race, sex, religion, color, or national origin. The ways that these cases are proven is basically through the use of statistics. For example, if more men than women are employed for a particular type of job, but an equal number of men and women, equally qualified, applied for that job type, it might be shown that the employer discriminates against women. The number of women employed by the employer is compared with the number of men employed in the pool of qualified persons for the job under review. Another example is the examination of a particular employment practice where the result is discrimination against a minority group. For example, the effect of a given requirement of employment may severely and disproportionately impact on hispanics as compared with caucasians.

Once disparate impact is shown, the employer has the burden of showing the challenged practice is: 1) directly related to job performance; and, 2) absolutely required in the operation of the business. If the employer cannot do this, his practices are unlawful.

Discrimination cases are difficult because resolution of the key issue usually boils down to whether the employer can show that the system or action the employee is disputing operates on objective as opposed to subjective criteria.

The EEOC has numerous regulations concerning the validity of common employment practices. The agency publishes criteria to which you can refer for guidance in specific situations. Go to your library and ask to see the *Uniform Guidelines and Employment Selection Procedures.* They are part of the *Congressional Federal Register.* Ask your librarian for 29 C.F.R. part 1607.

The key issue usually boils down to whether the employer can show the system operates on objective criteria.

Obtaining the "Right To Sue" Letter

Once an EEOC investigation is ended, the EEOC case worker makes findings and recommendations to management for review. If the district or area director of the EEOC finds *reasonable cause* to believe discrimination has occurred, the EEOC puts pressure on the employer to cure the discriminatory practice and may order the payment of damages or reinstatement of the aggrieved party. If this is unsuccessful, the case may be referred by the EEOC to the local U.S. Attorney for an action seeking to enforce the law.

If the EEOC finds no violation, the complainant is **not** prevented from suing. The complainant is given (by the EEOC) a *Right to Sue* letter which clears the way for the filing of a private lawsuit.

If the EEOC has not resolved your complaint within 180 days from the date you filed your original charge, you must request and obtain a *Right to Sue* letter (even though the matter is still unresolved at the EEOC level) before proceeding to court.

For more information, write for the booklet, *Information For The Private Sector and State and Local Governments*, and *Laws Enforced By The EEOC*, available free from the office of Communications and Legislative Affairs, EEOC, 1801 L Street, NW, Washington, D.C. 20507.

Age Discrimination in Employment Act of 1967 (ADEA)

The Age Discrimination Employment Act of 1967 (ADEA), found at 29 U.S.C. Section 621, bars age discrimination against those aged 40 or more. Like Title VII, almost every employer in the United States is covered. Like Title VII, there are severe penalties for employer retaliation against an employee filing any action based on this law. ADEA applies to all employers with 20 or more employees and all government workers. In addition to outlawing discrimination based on age, the Act specifically prohibits an employer from stopping or reducing the rate of pension benefit accruals because of age.

The OWBPA requires employers to prove the lawfulness of reducing benefits to older employees.

There is another law prohibiting age discrimination called The Older Worker's Benefit Protection Act (OWBPA), which became effective April 15, 1991. This act provides a number of supplementary provisions to the ADEA, and specifically makes all employee benefits and benefit plans subject to the anti-discrimination provisions of the ADEA. It also requires employers to prove the lawfulness of acts reducing benefits to older employees.

Filing an ADEA Complaint

Charges under ADEA or OWBPA must be filed with EEOC by or on behalf of an aggrieved person within 180 days of the discrimination. The aggrieved person's identity may be kept confidential. In states where there is a law prohibiting age discrimination, the complaint may be required to be filed with the state rather than federal agency. Check with your local EEOC office to find out more.

Like Title VII complaints, you must first file with the EEOC if you are claiming an ADEA violation in order to be eligible to file a private lawsuit in the courts against your employer. You cannot go to court first! If you do, the judge will throw your case out. If too much time has passed, it may be too late to file with the EEOC and you could lose both your right to file an EEOC complaint AND your right to sue your employer.

Sex Discrimination (Wages) Based on the Equal Pay Act.

The Equal Pay Act of 1963 (EPA), prohibits discrimination based on sex in payment of wages. In essence, it says that women and men performing substantially the same work for the same employer should be paid the same wage. Many employers who are too small (under 20 employees) or otherwise not subject to the rules of Title VII (relating to sex discrimination in general) are covered by EPA.

The EPA says that women and men performing the same work for the same employer should be paid the same.

Unlike Title VII and ADEA complaints, you are not required to file an EEOC complaint before filing civil suit directly against the employer. But be careful! Wage discrimination on account of sex may also be a Title VII violation **requiring** an EEOC filing before you have the legal right to sue in court. It is best to get expert legal advice in this situation. If an EPA charge is filed with EEOC, the investigation procedure is the same as outlined above.

A suit based on the EPA must be filed within two years (three years if a *willful or intentional* violation) of the discriminatory act. Filing an EEOC complaint does not stop the running of this time period.

If the EEOC finds reasonable cause to believe that an employer has violated the EPA and mediation fails, the EEOC may file suit on behalf of the victim in federal district court. If the EEOC files such an action, a private suit is not allowed.

The Employer's Defense(s)

The employer may not have to pay damages by proving there is a good reason for the pay difference.

Violations of the Equal Pay Act and Title VII of the Civil Rights Act of 1964 require a similar type of proof. The employee must show that the employer pays different wages for the same type of work. It is not necessary to prove that the employer *intended* to discriminate. However, the employer may defend the case and not have to pay damages by proving that there is a good reason for the difference in pay. The four accepted reasons for paying employees of a different sex different wages are:

- A seniority system

- A merit system

- A system that measures earnings by quantity or quality of production

- Some other difference based upon a factor other than sex

The employee can overcome these defenses if he can show that the system was really a pretext for intentional discrimination.

Please keep in mind that the Department of Labor is the agency charged with enforcing the Fair Labor Standards Act by civil action, but the Equal Pay Act is enforced and administered by the Equal Employment Opportunity Commission, 29 U.S.C. Section 106(d)(15).

If you intend to bring a suit under the Fair Labor Standards Act, be sure to keep accurate records of your wages earned and paid to you during in the time you have been employed, along with the type of tasks you are assigned as part of your employment.

Americans With Disabilities Act (ADA)

The Americans with Disabilities Act of 1990 (ADA) became law for employers of 25 or more on July 26, 1992. On July 26, 1994, the act will apply to employers of 15 employees or more. ADA is a significant addition to the law governing discrimination and provides significant new rights to millions of Americans. In the floor debates which preceded enactment, it was clear that many congressmen believed that discrimination based on disability was widespread, requiring comprehensive action.

The ADA, which can be found at 42 U.S.C. Section 12101 (also ask to see 29 C.F.R. part 1630) prohibits discrimination against those with disabilities in job application procedures, hiring, firing, job assignments, advancement, compensation, fringe benefits, job training and all other aspects of employment. One is disabled, as defined in the act, if he:

- has a physical or mental impairment that substantially limits a major life activity;

- has a record of such impairment; or

- is regarded as having such an impairment.

A disabled person may not be discriminated against in the workplace simply because of the disability

Anyone who is disabled may not be discriminated against in the workplace simply because of the disability. A *substantial* impairment is one which limits or restricts a major life activity such as

- hearing   • seeing

- speaking   • walking

- breathing   • caring for oneself

- working without devices or other aids

An employer may not ask a job applicant about his past or present disability-related medical condition or costs expended or expected to be expended in order to treat the disability. Nor can an employer require the applicant to take a medical examination, simply because he is disabled. However, a physical examination may be required if required of all the other applicants.

The employer has the burden of providing a work environment which does not present *substantial* physical obstacles to the disabled person's physical movement. All employees or applicants who satisfy the skill, experience, education and other job-related requirements of the position held or desired, and who, with *reasonable accommodation*, can perform the essential functions of that position, are entitled to be eligible for employment.

An employer must provide *reasonable accommodation* for an applicant or employee by:

- Making existing facilities accessible to and usable by the disabled

- Modifying or restructuring work assignments and schedules

- Modifying or installing additional equipment or devices necessary to help the employee carry out job duties

An employer is required to make all appropriate changes in the workplace in order to achieve *reasonable accommodation* of the disabled, unless the changes create *an undue hardship* in the operation of the business. *Undue hardship* is defined as that which causes an employer significant difficulty or expense when considered in light of factors such as the size of the business, the financial resources of the employer, the nature of the industry and structure of the business operation. An employer is not required to lower quality or production standards in order to accommodate a disabled person under the law, nor must the employer furnish

An employer is not required to lower quality standards in order to accommodate a disabled person.

personal use items such as eye glasses or hearing aids at his expense.

One who is qualified for the job and is able to perform the *essential functions* of employment (with reasonable accommodation supplied by the employer) cannot be refused the job simply because that person is disabled. The EEOC will consider the following factors in determining if a job function is essential:

- Whether the position exists primarily to do that function

- The number of other employees who could do this function

- The degree of expertise or skill necessary to do the function

The ADA does not require employers to actively seek out and hire disabled workers.

Further, the ADA prohibits an employer from refusing to hire an otherwise qualified individual who is disabled or who has a disabled dependent because it may cost more to insure this individual. However, the ADA does not create any affirmative action requirement on the part of an employer to actively seek out and hire disabled workers.

An employer can lawfully condition a job offer on the results of a medical examination, but only if all employees for the same or similar positions are required to undergo such an examination. The medical examination must be job-related or *consistent with business necessities*. The illegal use of drugs is not covered by ADA, even though drug addiction may create a sort of disability. Tests for illegal drug use are not subject to the medical examination restrictions.

ADA enforcement procedures and time requirements are the same for Title VII violations.

To receive more specific information about the contents of the ADA and how you can take advantage of this important law, contact the following organizations:

Office on the Americans with Disabilities Act,
Civil Rights Division
United States Department of Justice
P.O. Box 66118
Washington, D.C. 20035-6118
(202) 514-0301
(202) 514-0381, 0383 (TDD)

President's Committee for Employment of People with Disabilities
111 20th Street NW
Washington, D.C. 20210
(202) 653-5044
(202) 653-5050 (TDD)
Department of Transportation
400 7th Street SW
Washington, D.C. 20590
(202) 366-9305
(202) 755-7687 (TDD)

Disability and Business Technical Assistance Center
U.S. Dept. of Education
1-800-949-4232
National Organization on Disability
910 16th St. N.W., Suite 600
Washington, DC 20006
(202) 293-5960

ADAPT (American Disabled for Attendant Programs Today)
12 Broadway
Denver, CO 80203
(303) 733-9324

National Info. Center for Children and Youth with Disabilities
Box 1492
Washington, DC 20013
(800) 999-5599

The Disability Rights Education and Defense Fund (DREDF)
2212 6th Street
Berkeley, CA 94710
(800) 466-4ADA
(510) 644-2555

If you are interested in non-government publications about the ADA, I suggest:

The Disability Rag
$17.50/yr. (6 issues)
Box 145
Louisville, KY 40201

Kaleidoscope: International Magazine of Literature, Fine Arts, and Disabilities
$9/yr. (2 issues)
United Disability Services
326 Locust St.
Akron, OH 44320

Mainstream: Magazine of the Able-Disabled
$20/yr. (10 issues)
Box 370598
San Diego, CA 92137

Mouth: Voice of Disability Rights
$12/yr. (10 issues)
61 Brighton St.
Rochester, NY 14607

New Mobility
$18/yr. (6 issues)
1911 11th St. Suite 301
Boulder, CO 80203

Anti-Discrimination and Federal Contractors

Discrimination is the most significant evil the federal laws have been crafted to eliminate. Almost every aspect of federal law contains some specific anti-discrimination rule. In addition to the ADA, Title VII, ADEA, and EPA, if an employer holds a federal contract or subcontract, Executive Order 11246 prohibits job discrimination on the basis of race, color, sex, religion, or national origin. This is a far reaching law. It goes farther than the other federal anti-discrimination statutes by requiring affirmative action by employers who hold federal contracts to hire minority group members in order to insure equal opportunity in all aspects of employment.

Almost every aspect of federal law contains some specific anti-discrimination rule.

Similarly, Section 503 of the Rehabilitation Act of 1973 prohibits job discrimination because of a handicap, and also requires affirmative action on the part of federal contractors to employ in advance qualified disabled persons who, with reasonable accommodation, can perform essential job functions.

The Viet Nam Era Veterans Readjustment Assistance Act of 1974 (38 U.S.C. Section 4212), prohibits job discrimination by federal contractors against veterans and it too requires affirmative action by employers to employ or advance qualified Viet Nam war veterans.

Anyone who works for an employer doing business with the federal government has those additional rights. If you feel that you have been discriminated against or have not received effective affirmative action support from your employer who holds a federal contract or subcontract, you should contact the Office of Federal Contract Compliance Programs (OFCCP), Employment Standards Administration, U.S. Department of Labor, 200 Constitution Avenue, NW, Washington, D.C. 20210 (202) 523-9368, or an OFCCP regional or district office, listed in the blue pages in the telephone directory under *U.S. Government, U.S. Department of Labor*.

CHAPTER SEVEN
SEXUAL HARASSMENT

More women in the work place, changing cultural and societal values, and higher consciousness about sexual harassment all contribute to a heightened awareness of this issue. The Clarence Thomas hearings demonstrate the extent of the division of opinion in our country over what constitutes sexual harassment. The hearings also brought to light the unfortunate but widespread experience many women have had as victims of sexual harassment.

The most difficult task for courts in interpreting the laws prohibiting sex discrimination is defining what conduct amounts to sexual harassment. Although there is no precise definition, a number of important court decisions gives us some guidance.

> *The most difficult task for courts is defining what conduct amounts to sexual harassment.*

In a case called *Meritor Savings Bank v. Vinson,* 477 U.S. 57, 106 S.Ct. 2399, 40 F.E.P. 1822 (1986), the United States Supreme Court recognized two types of sexual harassment: *quid-pro-quo* and *hostile environment* harassment.

Quid-pro-quo sexual harassment is where an employee's advancement or financial well-being depends upon agreeing to some sort of unwelcome sexual advances. For example, the boss suggests an affair in exchange for a raise, a bonus or a better position. The boss also may suggest that failure to yield to his advances will cost the employee his job, a promotion, etc. If the advance is rejected, and the boss threatens, actually demotes or fires the worker, this unlawful *quid-pro-quo* sexual harassment has occurred.

Hostile Environment sexual harassment is more difficult to define. It generally refers to a work place environment where sexual advances, insensitive and unwelcome sexual innuendoes, or off-color jokes create an intimidating, offensive and difficult environment within which to work. Whether a hostile environment exists is decided by the courts on a case by case basis. For example, in the following cases a judge found a particular work place *hostile* due to sexual harassment and allowed money damages to be collected from the employer:

Whether a hostile work place environment exists is decided by the courts on a case by case basis.

> **Meritor Savings Bank v. Vinson (cited above). The boss had made repeated demands for sexual favors at work and after hours; he raped her; fondled her in front of others; exposed himself to her.**

> **EEOC v. Hacienda Hotel, 881 F.2d 1504 (9th Cir. 1989). The head of the engineering department at a hotel repeatedly made sexual comments and advances to the maids, whose female supervisor also called them derogatory sexual names.**

> **Hall v. Gus Construction, 842 F.2d 1010 (8th Cir. 1988). Male construction workers repeatedly fondled their female co-workers, showed them pornography, called them sexual names, exposed themselves and asked for sexual favors.**

If you feel you have been a victim of sexual harassment, your first recourse is to the EEOC by filing a Title VII complaint. You also have the right to sue your employer. The employer is always liable for damages if the harassment is the *quid-pro-quo* type, assuming that the person harassing is a supervisor or an actual agent, employee or owner of the firm.

If your claim is based on the *hostile environment* type of sexual harassment, the employer will be liable if 1) the employer knows of the problem or has reason to know of it and fails to take corrective action, or 2) the employer disregards the employee's complaints and has no reasonable policy or procedure for reviewing sexual harassment complaints.

Compensatory damages and punitive damages are awardable for sexual harassment. Generally, *compensatory* damages depend upon your state's law. Usually such damages are the amount of compensation awarded by a jury or judge that is reasonably necessary to compensate you for losses directly flowing from the defendant's act(s). Compensatory damages depend upon the nature and extent of the injury. The jury will award money for:

Compensatory damages and punitive damages are awardable for sexual harassment.

- The pain and suffering experienced and reasonably probable to be experienced in the future as a result of the injury;

- Reasonable expenses of medical care, treatment and services rendered and reasonably probable to be rendered in the future;

- Lost earnings to date and any decrease in earning power or capacity in the future;

- Loss of love, care, affection, companionship and other pleasures of marital or family relationship caused by the defendant's acts.

In addition to suing your employer for *compensatory* damages based on sexual harassment, you may be entitled to recover *punitive* damages as well. Whether punitive damages are available also depends upon your state's law, but generally, punitive damages are appropriate when the defendant's conduct is intentional, evil-minded or reckless. These damages are **not** related to your losses. Instead, the amount of a punitive award is based entirely on what the jury or the judge in your case thinks is necessary to punish the defendant, so as to deter him from repeating the same conduct in the future. Compensatory damages can be very small, while punitive damages can be very high, depending on how bad the conduct is.

> *Punitive damages are appropriate when the defendant's conduct is intentional, evil-minded or reckless.*

The Employer's Defenses

The defense in sexual harassment cases is usually based on some sort of consent or acquiescence by the employee. Employers' lawyers typically argue that any alleged sexual conduct was really simply consensual sex which just happened to involve the work place. On in the case of hostile environment case, that the conduct complained of was really tolerated or encouraged by this employee.

The courts generally hold that whether the sexual conduct is consensual or encouraged depends upon the facts in each case. Usually, sexual advances are considered unwelcome and not consensual if they are not desired by the receiver of the advance(s). What is *unwelcome* depends upon the point of view of the person who is receiving the advances. This standard is known to lawyers as the *reasonable woman standard* since more women than men have brought these type of cases. The standard asks, "would a reasonable woman, in the situation complained about, be offended to the point of feeling that her work environment was hostile?" The same test applies to men who are victims, substituting the word *men* for the word *women*.

If you feel you have been the victim of any sort of sexual harassment, report it at once to your employer, then to the EEOC. I also recommend that you contact a lawyer who handles both plaintiff's personal injury cases and labor cases, and who has experience representing employees in sexual harassment cases, to review the facts in your case.

Other Claims Against Your Employer For Sexual Harassment

You may have other claims against your employer or harassing supervisor besides sexual harassment and Title VII violations. What additional rights you have depend upon your state's laws. Each state has its own laws about *torts* or civil wrongs which also explain what kind of damages you are entitled to if you prove your claim. Other potential tort claims against your employer may be:

You may have other claims against your employer besides sexual harassment.

- Negligent hiring (if the employer knew or should have known of the supervisor's history of harassment in previous jobs);

- Intentional interference with contract (if the harassment prevents you from performing you work);

- Battery (if there is a harmful or offensive touching involved);

- False imprisonment (if you have been confined anywhere without your consent);

- Intentional infliction of emotional distress (where the conduct is outrageous).

See your lawyer about these—State laws are too dissimilar to intelligently summarize in a book this size. Your lawyer will plead those tort claims which are applicable in your case, in addition to whatever Title VII or discrimination claim you may have.

CHAPTER EIGHT
MY PLANT IS CLOSING—
WHAT ARE MY RIGHTS?
. . . .

The Federal Plant Closing Law provides that employers who employ 100 employees at a single site of employment must furnish 60 days advance written notice of a plant closing or a *mass layoff* to each of the following:

> *Employers who employ 100 at a single site must furnish 60 days advance written notice of a plant closing.*

- The union representative of the affected employees and each unrepresented employee

- The state's "dislocated worker's unit"

- The chief elected official of the affected locality.

A *mass layoff* is defined as a reduction in force during any 30 day period which results in an employment loss at that site of either: 1) 33% of the active employees (provided it affects at least 50 employees); or, 2) 500 employees at the site without regard to its percentage of overall number at the site.

A *plant closing* means a loss of employment by at least 50 employees, excluding part-time employees, at a single site or one or more facilities or operating units at that site during a 30 day period. The layoff must also exceed six months or result in a reduction of hours of more than 50% during each week.

Single site in employment is a key term in the plant closing law. To have a covered plant closing, or mass layoff, the number of affected employees must occur at the single site of employment. A single site of employment can be a single location or a group of separate buildings or areas not directly connected, but which are close to one another in distance and are used for the same purposes and share the same staff and equipment. This key term is not always easy to apply. For example, an office building with 50 different businesses may have 50 different sites of employment under the plant closing law—one for each employer's office present in the building. A corporation owning two plants located in different parts of the city and employing different workers in each plant may have two separate sites of employment, one for each of these plants.

Temporary projects, strikes and lockouts are outside of the plant closing law. There are also certain exceptions to the 60 day notice requirement available to employers under certain conditions. Under these exceptions, notice may be shortened. There are also special rules for relocation or consolidation of a business, for the sale of a business and where business circumstances caused a layoff whose length was not reasonably expected to be six months or more.

Temporary projects, strikes and lockouts are outside of the plant closing law.

To avoid evasion of the act, the Plant Closing Law also provides for a 90 day test period in which an employer must group employee losses over a 90 day period.

For each violation of the Plant Closing Law, the employer is responsible for back pay and benefits for each employee who did not receive the notice of the required length for each day that the notice requirement was not provided. There is a ceiling of 60 days. The employer may also be subject to fines of not more than $500 per day for each day that notice was not given in a timely way to local government. There are certain deductions which an employer may make to reduce his possible back pay and benefit obligations and eliminate the civil fine completely.

I suggest that you contact your union representative or a lawyer if your plant is closing to be sure that your rights are protected.

CHAPTER NINE
THE RIGHT TO ORGANIZE: LABOR UNIONS
· ·

National Labor Relations Act (NLRA)

The National Labor Relations Act (NLRA), also called the Wagner Act, was enacted in 1935. It was amended in 1947 and renamed the Labor Management Relations Act (LMRA) or the Taft-Hartley Act. Whenever you hear any of these names, you can be sure that the speaker is discussing the same law, which governs labor management relations in private industry throughout the United States. The agency which has been created to enforce the act is the National Labor Relations Board (NLRB). If you wish to read the Act, it is found at 29 U.S.C. Chapter 7.

The NLRA creates broad rights for employees to work through a union to negotiate wages and other benefits.

The key provision of the Act states:

Employees shall have the right to self-organization, to form, join or assist labor organizations, to bargain collectively through representatives of their own choosing, and to engage in other concertive activities for the purpose of collective bargaining or other mutual aid or protection and shall also have the right to refrain from any or all of such activities. . .

This section creates broad based rights for any employee to work through a union or other organization in order to negotiate wages and other benefits. An employer's violation of this section is governed under Section 8(a) of the Act, which sets forth the unfair labor practices which constitute violations of the Act. If you wish to

54

review these, look at 29 U.S.C. Section 158. Note also that Section 8(b) lists what is considered unfair labor practices by employee organizations.

Employer Violations of the Law

In essence, it is unlawful for any employer to interfere with, restrain or coerce employees in the exercise of their rights to join an employee organization or bargain collectively. An employer's mere threat to take retaliatory action against an employee engaging in organizing activity is also considered a violation, even if no action is taken by the employer.

It is also unlawful for an employer to dominate or interfere with the formation or administration of any labor organization. In other words, employers cannot encourage or contribute to any activity designed to prevent unionizing, including attempting to buy out the union by contributing to its finances. This is obviously designed to discourage employers from compromising the goals of the union and rendering its efforts on behalf of the employees ineffective.

It is also unlawful for an employer to encourage or discourage membership in any labor organization by discrimination in regard to hire or tenure of employment or any term or condition of employment. An employer cannot retaliate against an employee who has filed grievances. Retaliation carries severe penalties.

It is unlawful for an employer to discourage union membership by discrimination in regard to hire.

An employer violates the Act by refusing to bargain collectively with representatives of his employees. But the obligation to bargain collectively comes about only after the representatives of the employees have been chosen according to the terms of the Act. You are entitled to union representation if you are a member of the bargaining unit. Generally the bargaining unit consists of those employees with the same or similar interests. Most unions have extensive information available through their local offices. for more information about employer violations, contact your local union representative.

Employee Violations

It is unlawful for a union or other employee organization to restrain or coerce employees in the exercise of any of their rights or to restrain or coerce an employer in the selection of its representatives. However, any union may dictate conditions of membership and may enforce its own rules by fining members or even revoking membership for infractions of the rules.

Any union may dictate conditions of membership and may enforce its own rules by fining members.

It is an unfair practice for a union through its members to try to cause an employer to discriminate against an employee who is not a member of the union. In other words, the union is not to coerce workers to join, and it must represent all of the employees, regardless of whether the employees are not members of the union.

The law also prohibits the union from discriminating against its members on the basis of race, sex or religion, or on the basis of that individual's political activity within the union. The law also requires both unions and management to bargain with each other in good faith. There are literally thousands of cases which have been litigated in this area of the law. Please see a competent labor lawyer if you need more help with any problem you have with the union or other bargaining unit which represents you.

Employers Subject to the Law

The vast majority of employers are subject to the LMRA. However, the National Labor Relations Board has limited the applicability of the law to certain businesses. The Board has held that the law will not apply to retail establishments whose gross total sales are under $500,000. For non-retail businesses, the Board requires that the business follow the law if it has an *in-flow* of at least $50,000. An *in-flow* is defined as a direct or indirect purchase of goods from suppliers in other states.

The vast majority of employers are subject to the Labor Management Relations Act.

Assuming that the employer is covered under the act, then an employee will be protected unless the employee is a/an:

- "Employee" as defined in the Railway Labor Act (this is because these employees are protected by the Railway Labor Act, a separate labor law)

- Agriculture laborer

- Domestic worker

- Family employee (employees employed by a parent or spouse)

- Independent contractor

- Supervisor

If you have any concern about whether the LMRA applies to you, call your local NLRB office. You can find their numbers in the telephone book blue pages under *U.S. Government, Department of Labor.*

Enforcement Procedure

The NLRB deals with two types of cases: *R* cases and *C* cases. An *R* case involves issues concerning whether an employee wants to be represented by a particular union and the details of that representation.

C cases are unfair labor practice cases. *C* cases involve determining whether an employer or a union has violated some portion of the Taft-Hartley Act.

There is a strict procedural process which must be followed if you wish to enforce your rights under the Taft-Hartley Act. The procedure is outlined in detail in the U.S. Code and if you are interested in reviewing the statute, look under 29 U.S.C. Section 160. The rules enacted to carry out the statutory requirements are found at 29 C.F.R. Sections 102.9 to 102.59. Here are the steps:

- A charge is filed alleging a violation of the act with NLRB.

- The regional director of the Board assigns an agent to interview all of the persons who have knowledge about the matters in the charge.

- After the investigation has been completed, the regional director issues a complaint if he finds reasonable cause to believe there is a violation. If he finds no reasonable cause, he says so in writing.

- If the director finds cause, he then issues

a complaint which describes the violations.

- The employer or labor organization against which the complaint is made must respond within 10 days of the service of the complaint.

- A hearing is held, presided over by an administrative law judge of the National Labor Relations Board.

- The hearings are formal and the courtroom rules of evidence apply.

- After the hearing and legal arguments are made, the judge makes a decision supported by findings of fact and provides a recommendation to the NLRB.

- All parties then have a right to file exceptions (objections) to the decision of the administrative law judge.

- The entire record is then sent to the NLRB in Washington, D.C., which makes a decision agreeing with the judge or modifying or rejecting his recommendations.

The NLRB can order an employer or union to bargain in good faith or to stop doing the practice which has been found to be in violation of the Act (cease and desist order). NLRB can also require reinstatement of a discharged employee and award back pay. Court review of NLRB orders is also possible, but for this you will need a lawyer's help.

The NLRB can order an employer or union to bargain in good faith.

Labor-Management Reporting and Disclosure Act (LMRDA)

The Labor-Management Reporting and Disclosure Act (LMRDA) or Landrum-Griffith Act was passed in 1959. If you are interested in reading this act, look at 29 U.S.C. Section 401. The idea behind the law was to require reporting by both employers and unions of their activities as well as to regulate the internal administration of employee organizations. This law is usually not something that the average employee need be concerned with except for the union members' Bill of Rights, which is discussed below. The reporting and disclosure arguments create rights of notice to employees about management and union activities. A serious in-depth discussion about this aspect of the LMRDA is not warranted.

The idea behind the LMRDA is to require that both employers and unions report their activities.

The Bill of Rights for Members of Labor Organizations

The most important part of the LMRDA is the creation of a Bill of Rights for union members. After reviewing the Bill of Rights, if you feel that your rights have been violated, you should get an attorney; however, you may also file a complaint with the Labor-Management Services Administration (LMSA) without an attorney. If you decide to file a lawsuit, get a lawyer! Your suit must be filed in Federal District Court—not in your state's courts. Major provisions of the Bill of Rights can be categorized within five major areas: equal rights; freedom of speech and assembly; dues, initiation fees and assessments; protection of the right to sue; and safeguards against improper disciplinary action.

Equal rights

Every member has equal rights and privileges within the organization to: a) nominate candidates; b) vote in elections referenda of the organization; c) attend membership meetings; and, d) participate in such meetings subject to reasonable rules and regulations incorporated in the constitution or by-laws of the union.

Freedom of speech and assembly

Every member should have the right to meet with other members and to express any views, and to express at labor meetings his or her view upon business properly before the meeting, subject to established and reasonable rules pertaining to the conduct of meetings.

Dues, initiation fees and assessments

Dues, fees and assessments cannot be increased by a local labor organization except by a majority vote by secret ballot of the members in good standing; reasonable notice should be given each member of the section.

Dues cannot be increased by a local labor organization except by a majority vote by secret ballot.

Protection of the right to sue

No labor organization can limit the right of its members to institute an action in court or before an administrative agency, except that the union by its constitution or by-laws may require that the individual exhaust reasonable hearing procedures within the framework of that organization.

Safeguards against improper disciplinary action

Most important to the union member is his right not to be fined, suspended, expelled, or otherwise disciplined by a labor organization unless and until he has been:

- Served with written specific charges;

- Given a reasonable time to prepare a defense; and

- Afforded a full and fair hearing.

The one exception to this right allows the union to discipline a member for non-payment of dues without providing the safeguards mentioned above.

Collective Bargaining Agreements

Collective Bargaining Agreements are governed by the Taft-Hartley Act. If you wish to read the part of the law which concerns collective bargaining, look at 29 U.S.C. Section 129(a). This section provides:

> **... representatives designated or selected for the purposes of collective bargaining by the majority of the employees in a union appropriate for such purposes shall be the exclusive representatives of all the employees in such unit for the purpose of collective bargaining in respect to rates of pay, wages, hours of employment, or other conditions of employment.**

The collective bargaining section of the Taft-Hartley Act instills a duty of good faith for both the employer and union.

This section clearly establishes that the union is the only appropriate and legal representative of the employees for the purpose of bargaining.

This law does not state what the terms of any collective bargaining agreement should be. It simply instills a duty of good faith for both the employer and union during the course of bargaining. It also very generally describes the issues important to each side such as wages, hours, and working conditions. Strikes or lock-outs are permissible under certain circumstances.

The idea behind the law is not to influence the terms of the contract, but to provide a procedural vehicle for the employer and employees to come to some sort of agreement. When both sides agree, the agreement becomes the declaration of all the rights that the employee has with the employer. In essence it becomes the contract of employment between worker and employer.

Pursuant to this law, the union still remains the exclusive representative of the employee even after the agreement is signed. This is true even if you are not in the union. The contract must contain a grievance procedure. Get a copy of the agreement! It will outline what you may do as an aggrieved employee in order to enforce the rights you were given under the agreement, whether you are a member of the union or not.

The usual method of enforcement of the rights created in the collective bargaining agreement is a grievance procedure, resulting in some sort of arbitration (non-court procedure) which binds the parties. However, the union itself is usually the only party (not you or another union member or non-member) which can file a grievance and submit a dispute to arbitration.

The most effective solution to a problem is to contact the union representative, even if you are not a member.

If you find yourself with a problem, even though you are not a member of the union, your most effective solution is to contact the union representative and request that the union file a grievance for you. The law confers very broad discretion on the union as to which cases they choose to process your grievance. If you are unhappy with the union's action, you may file an unfair labor charge. You may have grounds for a suit based upon breach of duty of fair representation, which constitutes a violation of the Taft-Hartley Act. Again, first contact your local office of the Department of Labor for more information. Then consult a private lawyer.

CHAPTER TEN
EMPLOYEE BENEFITS

The Employee Retirement Income Security Act of 1974 (ERISA)

Perhaps you have heard of an important law called ERISA. If you would like to read it, it is found at 29 U.S.C. Section 2001. The concept behind this law is to protect employees who are included in their employer's retirement plans. This act tells employers what they can and cannot do with the money that is paid into an employee pension benefit plan.

> *The concept behind ERISA is to protect employees who are included in their employer's retirement plans.*

Employment pension benefit plans include all employee benefit plans which are kept by an employer and which are designed to provide retirement and income to employees.

There are two types of pension benefit plans. The first is a *Defined Benefits Plan*, which basically promises to provide a specific benefit at the time when an employee retires or in a certain period of time after retirement. The second type is a *Defined Contribution Plan*, which provides an individual account for the employee based upon the amount contributed to the plan, plus any earnings and losses.

ERISA applies to employee welfare benefit plans, which include health, vacation, sick pay, day care, pre-paid legal services, severance pay and death benefit plans. Since ERISA is an extremely complicated statute, **YOU MUST GET PROFESSIONAL HELP IN THIS AREA IF**

YOU HAVE A PROBLEM WITH EMPLOY-MENT RETIREMENT BENEFITS.

Keep in mind that the purpose of the law is to keep employers from mishandling, misusing or misapplying the funds which are kept in these accounts. Since employers keep the records and get certain tax advantages for contributing to these plans, it is always tempting for an employer to use this money for something other than for the employees' benefit.

It is always tempting for an employer to use retirement funds for something other than the employees' benefit.

So the law imposes extensive reporting and disclosure requirements, such as:

- special forms must be filed by the employer with the IRS to obtain favorable tax treatment;

- a notice of a plan's termination must be filed with the IRS;

- each plan is supposed to have an administrator who is responsible for keeping accurate, precise records;

- each year the plan administrator must file an annual report describing what has happened with the money in the fund;

- a copy of this report, or summary of it, must be distributed to all participants, including the employees;

- the plan administrator must file a summary of the plan with the Department of Labor when the plan is first established;

- all employees who participate in the plan must be given a copy of the summary within three months of when the plan takes effect or when they become covered by the plan;

- employers must provide summaries of any modifications to the plan within 210 days after the close of the plan year when the changes were made;

- notice of any amendment which decreases the benefit which would be paid to the employee must be given to the employee no later than fifteen days before the effective date of the amendment;

- the plan administrator must copy all records related to the plan and provide them to plan participants upon request.

Before ERISA took effect, employees sometimes failed to receive pension benefits when they quit their employment because the employer told them they were not *vested*. A pension plan *vests* when the employee has a right to the benefits under the program. The ERISA law establishes a vesting schedule for employer contributions which involve set periods of between 0 and 7 years. As a result of this law, the employer no longer has complete discretion to set the time of vesting. Maximum vesting periods are now established by law.

As a result of ERISA, the employer no longer has complete discretion with respect to vesting of retirement plans.

Once an employee has vested rights in his plan, he must be paid his benefits no later than (1) at the completion of ten years of service, (2) at the age of 65, or, (3) when the employment is terminated.

ERISA requires that all of these benefits be paid in the form of a joint and survivor annuity (payment over time) unless both the employee and the spouse give up this provision. If an employee dies before he retires, the plan must pay an annuity to the surviving spouse on the date when the deceased would first have been eligible for retirement. The ERISA law protects employees in the following ways:

If an employee dies before he retires, the plan must pay an annuity to the surviving spouse.

- Benefits cannot be assigned (except by court order).

- Defined benefit plans must meet specific funding standards insuring solvency of the plan.

- There are specific fiduciary duties set out for plan administrators making them personally liable if the plan is not managed properly.

- Insurance is provided automatically by a Pension Benefit Guarantee Corporation, which insures the payout of the benefits accrued over the years.

For more information on your pension and how to protect it, contact:

Public Affairs
Pension Benefit Guarantee Corporation
2020 K St., NW, Room 7100
Washington, DC 20006-1860
(202) 778-8840

The Consolidated Omnibus Budget and Reconciliation Act of 1985 (COBRA)

The Consolidated Omnibus Budget Reconciliation Act of 1985 (COBRA) is a law designed to permit an employee to remain a member of an employer group health plan after his employment is terminated. If an employee takes advantage of this law, he will be covered for health benefits, but the employee must pay for the health coverage himself.

COBRA applies to employers with more than 20 employees. For employees subject to this act, the medical coverage begins on the date the coverage would otherwise end due to termination of employment. The law requires that employees be allowed to buy continuation coverage for up to 18 months if coverage is lost because of termination or reduction in hours. Otherwise, employees or other beneficiaries can purchase coverage for up to three years from the date of the expiration of the original coverage.

COBRA requires that employees be allowed to buy continuation coverage for up to 18 months.

You may be entitled to continuation coverage if one of the following happens to you:

- You lose your job for any reason, even if it is negligence on your part (the only exception is gross or reckless misconduct).

- Reduction in hours

- Death of the employee who is your spouse

- Divorce or legal separation

- Eligibility for Medicare

- Loss of status as a dependent child

If you quit your job, you would be entitled to 18 months of continuation coverage under the act. The law also permits you to elect coverage for a period less than the COBRA minimum, but in no case can you get continuation coverage beyond 36 months. Other reasons for your continuation coverage ending include:

- The employer stops providing health coverage to employee

- You become delinquent in payment of the continuation premium

- You become covered under a new group health plan

- You become entitled to Medicare

How Do I Get COBRA Coverage?

The law requires that each employee and beneficiary (for example your son or daughter who is qualified as a beneficiary in your original policy with your employer) be provided with continuation coverage which is of the same type which was provided under the original employer's health plan. But you pay the premiums—not your employer. You are entitled to continuation coverage even if there is some problem with your health when your employment ends. Benefits are not dependent upon you providing the insurance carrier with some evidence of being a good risk. You are guaranteed coverage once you make the election.

You are entitled to continuation coverage even if there is some problem with your health when your employment ends.

If you elect to take continuation coverage, you will get all the benefits (and be subject to all the limitations) which would apply to participants in the employment group plan during the same period. In other words, the original group policy restrictions and reductions in coverage will apply to your continuation coverage. Similarly, if the other employees in the original plan are given an option for coverage modification or open enrollment, you will also have these same opportunities. Please remember, COBRA gives you this right to extend health coverage after your employment ends provided you, not your employer, pay the premiums. COBRA won't help you if you can't pay the premiums.

Employer Requirements Under COBRA

COBRA requires the employer to provide written notification to any newly terminated employee and his spouse of their option to continue coverage. Your employer must tell you of this right and the right of your beneficiaries to elect continuation coverage within 14 days of your termination. You and your beneficiaries then have 60 days from the date you received notice of the COBRA continuation rights to elect coverage. If you do not tell your benefits clerk, plan administrator or the person in charge of administrating the health plan benefits at your place of employment within 60 days that you intend to elect coverage, you lose all of your rights under COBRA.

You have 60 days from the date you received notice of COBRA rights to elect coverage.

Please keep in mind that you or your qualified beneficiary must tell your employer or plan administrator if you or a former dependent loses eligibility because of divorce, legal separation, loss of dependent child status, etc. You must tell your employer or plan administrator of these changes in circumstances within 60 days of the event giving rise to your loss of coverage. If you do not do this, the qualified beneficiaries will lose their rights to elect any continuation coverage.

Employer Penalties Under COBRA

If your employer violates COBRA, he is subject to an excise tax of: 1) $100 per day for each COBRA violation to an employee or qualified beneficiary; or, 2) $200 per day for multiple COBRA violations involving family members arising out of the same qualifying event. In addition, plan administrators may be liable if they are personally responsible for the COBRA violations.

Under certain conditions, plan administrators may be personally liable for COBRA violations.

Since this is a very complex area, an attorney should be consulted. However, if you need more information before contacting an attorney, contact the U.S. Department of Labor Pension and Welfare Benefits Administration at:

U.S. Department of Labor
Pension and Welfare Benefits Administration
Division of Technical Assistance and Inquiries
200 Constitution Ave., NW (Room N-5658)
Washington, D.C. 20210

If you are a government employee, the COBRA rules are slightly different. Obtain information about federal COBRA law details from:

U.S. Public Health Service
Office of the Assistant Secretary for Health
Grant's Policy Branch (COBRA)
5600 Fisher's Lane (Room 17A-45)
Rockville, Maryland 2085

Each of these agencies will be able to provide you with an excellent pamphlet produced by the United State Government Printing Office called *Health Benefits Under the Consolidated Omni-*

bus Budget Reconciliation Act (COBRA). It will be provided to you upon request, free of charge.

Worker's Compensation

Worker's or Workman's Compensation law is not governed by federal law. Each state has its own workman's compensation act. Generally, worker's compensation acts provide money or benefits to employees who suffer physical, mental or emotional injuries from accidents arising from their employment. The employer pays the insurance premiums necessary for covering all of his employees and as a result, any employee who is hurt while acting in the course and scope of his employment is provided with insurance benefits for the injury according to his state's law. The amount of money or benefits paid out is dictated by a schedule established by state statute.

Worker's Compensation provides money to employees who suffer physical or emotional injuries arising from their employment.

Some states give the employee the option to choose whether he wants to be covered by workman's compensation when he starts work for the employer. Other worker's compensation acts are mandatory for all employers; that is, the employer has no choice. In those states which allow employees to opt out of coverage and the employee makes such an election, the employee will not be entitled to any benefits under the worker's compensation act if hurt on the job. Once you are covered, your rights cannot be forfeited.

Worker's compensation law provides the only remedy for work-related accidents. In other words, in exchange for your employer providing insurance coverage for you in case you are hurt on the job, you are legally prohibited from suing your employer (except where the opt-out election is taken, if your state allows this procedure or in very limited circumstances, usually involving intentional wrongdoing by your employer).

If your state allows you to opt out of worker's compensation coverage, thereby allowing you to sue your employer directly, you will not be entitled to worker's compensation benefits. And if you fail to prove that your employer was at fault for your work-related injury, you will receive no benefits whatsoever. Opting out of the system is rare. You are probably covered by worker's compensation and therefore entitled to benefits if you are hurt on the job.

You do not have to prove that someone caused your work-related injury in order to collect.

The worker's compensation system is a "no fault" system of benefits. This means that you do not have to prove that someone caused your work-related injury or that you were without fault in order to collect. Why the injury happened or whether you were negligent in causing or contributing to your injury at work is irrelevant to receiving benefits.

Benefits available through Workman's Compensation are of two types: 1) medical payments for expenses related to health care including doctors, hospitals, prescriptions and physical therapy; and 2) disability payments for lost wages due to the injury. Disability payments are either *temporary* or *permanent*; *total* or *partial*.

Temporary total payments are made when an injured worker cannot return to work, is still treating for his injury, and the treating doctor has specified "no work" status. Each state has a cap on benefits. For example, in Arizona these benefits are paid every two weeks at two-thirds of the employee's average monthly wage, capped by statute at $210 per month.

Temporary partial disability payments are made when the worker is released to light or full work status before his medical treatment ends. This benefit, in Arizona for example, is calculated at two-thirds of the difference between the worker's average monthly wage and the wage he is able to earn according to his release status. Your state's benefits may be different.

Permanent disability payments are either partial or total and are not paid until the employee's condition is medically stable. This means that the condition is not getting any better or any worse. The American Medical Association has published guidelines for physicians to use in order to determine when a permanent medical condition is total or partial. The courts rely on these guidelines in fixing benefits.

Permanent disability payments are not paid until the employee's condition is medically stable.

Permanent disability is either "*scheduled*" or "*unscheduled.*" Scheduled means that your injury involves something related to a typical or "routine" injury, usually involving sight or extremities. Unscheduled injuries are more complicated. Unscheduled injuries relate to the impact on the functioning of the entire person, and are not related to the extremities or sight. These are evaluated on a case by case basis.

Unscheduled cases usually involve back, hip, neck, shoulder or mental or emotional injuries. Permanent benefits are paid only when the worker's future earning capacity is affected. As you might guess, the distinction between scheduled and unscheduled classification is a source of great conflict between the workman's compensation insurance carrier and the worker.

Generally, filing a claim is easy. You or your employer or your treating physician report the industrial injury to your state agency which administers your workman's compensation law. The state agency reports it to the workman's compensation insurance carrier which has a short period (usually 10 to 30 days) within which to decide whether to accept or deny the claim. If accepted, the doctors' fees are paid and any disability payments are made according to a fee schedule set by state law.

Workman's compensation claims are paid according to a schedule set by state law.

Here are some tips if you have suffered an injury at work or while doing some task for your employer:

Report it to your employer immediately. This is because most states have short statutes of limitations, usually one year, which require the reporting to be done within this period or the claim is lost forever;

Get medical treatment immediately and tell your doctor that you were hurt at work;

If you disagree with a "Notice of Claim Status" issued by the workman's compensation carrier or self-insured employer, get a lawyer who specializes in workman's compensation cases and fight!

Any complaint that you have about your workman's compensation benefits must be routed through your state agency. The agency will issue a finding and an award. In Arizona, for example, recourse is through the Arizona State Industrial Commission. The Industrial Commission conducts hearings, and makes rulings. These orders are enforceable against the carrier and the worker. After your state agency processes your claim and makes its decision, the insurance carrier is then required to pay the benefits set by your state law for that category of injury. Appeals are governed by your state's laws.

If you have already filed a workman's compensation claim and have been paid for it and you have a new or previously undiscovered condition that is related to the original work-related injury, you can petition to re-open your claim. This is your right for your entire life.

However, in order to win any case you will have to prove, usually through strong medical testimony, that your condition has worsened, or that there are good reasons for you not to have discovered your present complaint earlier. I strongly suggest that you hire a lawyer who specializes in workman's compensation cases. Similarly, if you are hurt at work and your employer has no workman's compensation coverage or is not a duly authorized self-insurer, you have a considerably more valuable claim, since there are severe state penalties for employers who do not carry workman's compensation insurance when it is required by law.

There are severe state penalties for employers who do not carry workman's compensation insurance when required by law.

Since workman's compensation law is governed by your state's particular statutes and cases interpreting these laws, you must obtain a lawyer's help in this area to get all that you are entitled to. Not only is each state's law a bit different, but the procedural rules which govern how a claim is processed also vary from state to state. Don't be deterred from hiring a lawyer due to lack of funds, because most, if not all, workmen's compensation lawyers will represent you on a contingency fee basis (see page 4) rather than an hourly fee basis.

> *Most workmen's compensation lawyers will represent you on a contingency fee basis.*

If you are employed by the Federal Government, there is a worker's compensation program established by federal statute which applies to you. The federal system is similar to the state system but for more information about federal worker's compensation, write:

Office of Worker's Compensation Programs
Federal Employees' Compensation Division
Employment Standards Administration
Department of Labor
200 Constitution Ave., NW, Room S-3229
Washington, DC 20210
(202) 523-7552

Veterans' Rights

A number of federal and state laws provide re-employment rights to military veterans, including reservists. The laws generally encourage employment and promotion of veterans. However, the law allows an employer to refuse to re-employ a veteran if the employer can establish that conditions have changed to such an extent that it is impossible or unreasonable to re-employ or advance the veteran.

Generally a veteran is entitled to his *rightful place* in the workplace after he has completed his service obligation and requested re-employment.

The veteran is supposed to be placed in the job he would have had were it not for his military service. The returning veteran must seek re-employment within 90 days of his release from active duty.

A veteran's job is secure for one year following re-employment, unless the employer can prove that there is just cause for discharge. Importantly, seniority and benefits tied to seniority are protected for the returning veteran. Thus, a veteran's seniority continues and builds during his period of military service. So, at the time of re-employment, he will be able to enjoy the fruits of the accumulated seniority.

A veteran's seniority continues and builds during his period of military service.

There are a comprehensive set of federal rights and benefits for veterans and their dependents which are too numerous to discuss in this publication. If you are interested in learning about all of the rights to which a veteran and his dependents are entitled, contact:

Department of Veterans' Affairs
Office of Public Affairs
810 Vermont Avenue, NW
Washington, D.C. 20420

You may also wish to contact your local Veteran's Administration office, the number for which is listed in the blue pages under *United States Government, Veteran's Administration* or you may call the nationwide toll free number, 1-800-669-8477, between 8:00 a.m. and 5:30 p.m., eastern time. The best single publication dealing with federal benefits for veterans and dependents is produced by the United States Government Printing Office and is available to you free of charge. Write to the Department of Veteran's

Affairs, at the address above, and request the pamphlet called *Federal Benefits for Veterans and Dependents*. As of this printing, the newest edition is January, 1991.

Unemployment Compensation Benefits

Please keep in mind that all unemployment compensation is governed by state and not federal law. As you might guess, each state's law is different regarding eligibility requirements and benefits.

There tend to be some common threads in every state's unemployment compensation system. Generally, an employee who quits his job voluntarily and without good cause, will lose whatever rights he has to unemployment compensation benefits. By sharp contrast, employees who are laid off will qualify for benefits.

Generally, an employee who quits his job without good cause loses his right to unemployment compensation benefits.

Typical disqualifying conditions include termination for willful or negligent conduct; refusing suitable work; making false statements to the state agency administering unemployment benefits.

Generally, if you are eligible for benefits, you will receive a benefit proportionate to your earning level at your last job. There is a limit, however. The benefits are capped at a certain amount set by state statute (regardless of an employee's earnings before the end or break in active employment).

If you believe that you are eligible for benefits, file promptly with the appropriate state agency. If your claim is denied, find out about your appeal rights. Often, you must appeal quickly, in writing, and to a certain governmental agency, or your appeal rights will be lost. Maintain your job search at all times in order to establish that you are, in good faith, looking for work for which you are qualified.

To find out more, look in the telephone directory blue pages for *State Government* under *Department of Economic Security, Unemployment Compensation*, etc.

CHAPTER ELEVEN
THE RIGHT TO A SAFE
AND HEALTHY WORKPLACE

Both federal and state laws seek to promote safety in the workplace. Protection comes either from federal Occupational Safety and Health Administration (OSHA) rules or an OSHA approved state program meeting OSHA's standards.

Federal and state safety laws are designed to reduce hazards in the workplace, improve safety training, and provide a reporting system to record workplace injuries. These laws also provide employees with a number of other rights. To review the OSHA law, refer to 29 U.S.C. Section 651.

OSHA requires all employers to furnish a place of employment which is free from recognized hazards.

OSHA requires all employers to furnish a place of employment which is free from recognized hazards that cause or are likely to cause death or serious harm. The United States Department of Labor has the primary responsibility for administering the act. OSHA sets occupational safety and health standards, and its Compliance Safety and Health Officers (CSHO's) conduct job site inspections to help insure compliance with the act.

OSHA requires that a representative of the employees be given an opportunity to accompany an OSHA inspector to the job site for the purpose of pointing out any workplace safety or health problems.

Citations issued by USDL to the employer for safety violations must be posted so that employees are informed of them. If the employer challenges a citation, employees must be advised and informed of the hearing date.

An employee may also request an investigation by USDL if he believes that there are unsafe or hazardous conditions in the workplace, or the employee may file a complaint with USDL. A reporting employee is protected from retaliation by a portion of the OSHA law which establishes severe penalties for employers who retaliate against employees who exercise OSHA rights.

A reporting employee is protected by OSHA law, which establishes severe penalties for employers who retaliate.

Employees who believe they have been punished because of a report made against the employer must file a complaint with USDL within 30 days. USDL will investigate and, if the charges have merit, USDL will seek to undo the recriminatory act, including through the U.S. Department of Justice in the courts. Reinstatement and back pay are also available.

OSHA provides for mandatory civil penalties against employers of up to $7,000 for each serious violation and for optional penalties of up to $7,000 for each non-serious violation. Penalties of up to $7,000 per day may be proposed for failure to correct violations within a proposed time period and for each day the violation continues beyond the prescribed abatement date.

Further, any employer who willfully violates the act may be assessed penalties of up to $70,000 for each such violation. A minimum penalty of $5,000 may be imposed for each willful violation. A violation of posting requirements can bring a penalty of up to $7,000.

There are also criminal penalties in OSHA. For example, any willful violation resulting in the death of any employee is punishable by a fine of up to $250,000 (or $500,000 if the employer is a corporation), or by imprisonment for up to six months, or both. A second conviction of an employer doubles the possible term of imprisonment. Falsifying records, reports, or applications is punishable by a fine of $10,000 or up to six months in jail or both.

Several states impose criminal penalties on corporations that fail to warn employees at risk in a timely manner.

Several states impose criminal penalties on corporations or corporate managers if they know of serious concealed dangers, do not warn employees at risk in a timely manner, and either fail to cure the problem or notify the employees or state labor department about the risk. Check with your local state's attorney, County Attorney, or Attorney General for more information.

While providing penalties for safety and health violations, OSHA also encourages efforts by labor and management, before an OSHA inspection, to voluntarily reduce workplace hazards and to develop and improve safety and health programs. To report suspected fire hazards, imminent danger, safety and health hazards in the workplace, or other job safety and health emergencies, such as toxic waste in the workplace, call USDL's 24-hour hotline: 1-800-321-OSHA.

If you want to learn more about this area of the law, the government has published safety and health program management guidelines to assist employers in establishing or developing programs to prevent or control employee exposure to workplace hazards which are available from the nearest regional office near you. Regional office phone numbers are:

Atlanta, GA	**(404) 347-3573**
Kansas City, MO	**(816) 426-5861**
Boston, MA	**(617) 565-7164**
New York, NY	**(212) 337-2378**
Chicago, IL	**(312) 353-2220**
Philadelphia, PA	**(215) 596-1201**
Dallas, TX	**(214) 767-4731**
San Francisco, CA	**(415) 744-6670**
Denver, CO	**(303) 844-3061**
Seattle, WA	**(206) 442-5930**

To report an accident, unsafe condition in your workplace or any unfair conduct on the part of your employer related to OSHA, contact:

Office of Field Programs
Occupational Safety
and Health Administration
Department of Labor
200 Constitution Ave., NW, Room N-3603
Washington, DC 20210
(202) 523-7725

Sick Buildings

Perhaps you have read or heard about workers who have experienced chronic sickness at work. Maybe you have yourself suffered from a chronic illness while at the workplace. Complaints vary, but often workers suffer from symptoms similar to allergic reactions, which may include headaches, chronic respiratory problems, and fainting spells. Symptoms are usually predominantly prevalent during or shortly after work. See a doctor immediately if you are suffering from discomfort of any kind while on the job.

Studies suggest a link between workers' sickness and indoor pollution caused by inadequate ventilation; dirty air filters; toxic building materials; toxic exhaust from office machines like copiers, shredders and facsimiles; contaminated drain pans; pesticide use near ventilating system vents; secondary tobacco smoke. Whether your workplace is causing your harm depends upon the conclusions of your doctor and experts on toxins, ventilation and building materials. This is a complex problem. A starting point and good rule of thumb is that a minimum of 20 cubic feet per minute of fresh outdoor air per person is required to maintain a healthy indoor environment even if there is no problem with toxic building materials and machine caused toxins. If your illness is work-related, your medical expenses and disability benefits should be paid by worker's compensation. You may have a suit against your employer if he intentionally fails to remedy the problem, after having notice of it. You may also have claims against the owner of the building and/or manufacturers of the products causing the problem.

This a relatively new area of litigation and much work needs to be done in establishing standards and defining the actual causes or contributing factors of chronic employee sickness. The National Institution for Occupational Safety and Health (NIOSH) investigates sick building complaints. Its hot line number is (800) 35-NIOSH. NIOSH also provides basic information and referrals to state and local health de-

> *Studies suggest a link between workers' sickness and indoor pollution caused by inadequate ventilation.*

partments. You may want to contact them directly at:

National Institute for Occupational Safety and Health
4676 Columbia Parkway
Cincinnati, OH 45226
(800) 356-4674

In addition, the Public Information Center of the Environmental Protection Agency (EPA) publishes a list of experts in the field who are skilled at determining whether your workplace is causing or contributing to your poor health. Call or write either:

EPA
Washington, D.C. 20460
(202) 260-2080

Air Quality Office
EPA
Washington, D.C. 20460
(202) 233-9030

The EPA's publication, *Building Air Quality: A Guide For Building Owners and Facility Managers*, explains how to prevent and clean up indoor air pollution and costs $24.00. Order it from:

New Orders
Superintendent of Documents
P.O. Box 371954
Pittsburgh, PA 15250-7954
Order by Fax: (202) 512-2250

You may also wish to contact the American College of Occupational & Environmental Medicine at (708) 228-6850 or the Association of Occupational & Environmental Clinic at (202) 347-4976, for names of health care providers in your area who specialize in indoor pollution diagnosis and treatment.

Smoking in the Workplace

There is no blanket federal law forbidding smoking in the workplace with the exception of the Federal Aviation Administration (FAA) rules prohibiting smoking on domestic flights. If you are a travel agent or other airline employee who flies and the airline has refused to enforce the FAA ban on non-smoking, you may be entitled to workmen's compensation benefits for medical treatment, lost wages and disability payments if your medical condition is related to secondary smoke in an airplane. You may also have a claim against your airline employer for intentionally failing to maintain a safe and healthy workplace. Under most state worker's compensation laws, such a suit would first require that you show that your airline employer knew of the violations of the FAA anti-smoking rules and intentionally disregarded their enforcement. (See the discussion about worker's compensation on page 73).

Some states and many cities regulate smoking in government buildings and privately owned facilities.

Some states and many cities and towns regulate smoking in government buildings and privately owned facilities such as restaurants. For example, as of March 1, 1993, California law prohibits smoking in all buildings owned or leased by the state, including hospitals and prisons. California is the eighth state to mandate smoke free government buildings. Colorado, Delaware, Idaho, Maryland, Massachusetts, Michigan and Vermont have similar laws.

If you work in an environment where secondary smoke creates a health hazard, in addition to a possible workmen's compensation claim, you may have an OSHA claim as well. Your doctor must be prepared to testify that the secondary smoke at work is the cause of your present health problem.

Smoking is a creation of local law. To learn about the laws in your area, start with the State or County Attorney or Attorney General. Also, call the office of your city or town attorney. They should be able to supply you with a copy of the law and tell you if it is enforced. Keep in mind that regardless of what the laws provide, your employer may have a policy about smoking. Ask for a copy of the rules and be sure to report any infraction to him. Failure to enforce may be grounds for legal action.

CHAPTER TWELVE
THE EMPLOYEE'S RIGHT TO PRIVACY

Every individual is afforded a right to be free from unreasonable searches and seizures by virtue of the Fourth and Fourteenth Amendments to the United States Constitution. However, these rights are rights the citizen has against the government. These rights do not prevent a co-worker or your employer from searching your things at work, unless the employer is a government agency. That is, the Constitution protects people from unreasonable searches and seizures conducted by the government only: as a government worker, you have much greater protection than your private sector counterpart. The Constitution says nothing about unreasonable searches conducted by our fellow citizens or our private, non-governmental employers. When an employee agrees to perform services as an employee for an employer at the employer's place of business, does the employee retain any rights of privacy? As you will see, there are a number of interesting areas that merit discussion.

> *The Constitution says nothing about unreasonable searches conducted by private, non-governmental employers.*

Drug Testing

Drug testing remains a very controversial issue in the law. It is invasive. That is, it's a kind of search that is unconstitutional if performed by the government without consent. Some employers have instituted mandatory drug testing. Numerous cases have tested whether an employee is required to participate in drug testing or screening. Although there is some variation in the law from state to state and between different federal courts, some generalizations are possible.

First, random drug testing is generally *not* allowed, and it is viewed with the most suspicion by the courts. However, if the employer can demonstrate a compelling business justification for random drug testing, such as serious and substantial safety considerations, random drug testing may be permissible under certain circumstances. The nature of the employer's industry and the nature of the work being performed by the employee are the most important variables. The more sensitive the work performed and the more delicate or exacting the type of business, the more likely the courts are to allow drug testing.

If the employer can demonstrate a compelling business justification, random drug testing may be permissible.

Public employees have more protection from random drug testing and drug screening because of the more liberal rights given to federal employees. Your state's constitution may provide additional rights beyond the protections discussed previously.

Secondly, we can generalize that applicants tend to have less protection than employees who are already on the payroll. In other words, an employer may require drug testing of an applicant as a condition of employment. The theory is that by making this a condition which the applicant can reject, the applicant is consenting to the test or waiving any right to claim that the testing is an unreasonable search. He has the choice not to submit, but in reality, a refusal to submit usually means an end to his hopes for the job. The bottom line on random testing is that it is not supported by the courts unless the job or business is somewhat special. (An example might be a drug manufacturer employer who has access to drugs and is also responsible for carefully labeling the drugs.)

Individualized or reasonable suspicion testing based on objective factors tends to be viewed more favorably by the courts. That is, where an employer has some objective evidence of drug use among the work force, courts are likely to allow the employer to conduct some kind of reasonable drug testing. For example, if an employee has slurred speech, glazed eyes, an unsteady gait or difficulty in communicating, a supervisor may be justified in suspecting the employee's fitness for duty. Similarly, if the supervisor is concerned about the employee correctly operating machinery, or otherwise fulfilling employment related tasks because of drug or alcohol impairment, courts are likely to uphold tests, provided the testing is: 1) based on a reasonable belief that the employee is under the influence; 2) done at a reasonable time and place; and 3) done in the least intrusive manner as possible.

Where an employer has evidence of drug use among the work force, courts are likely to allow some kind of drug testing.

For those employers who have a drug testing or screening program, the procedures associated with their program must be the same in every case. In other words, the drug testing or screening must conform to the employer's stated drug testing policy, and the policy should be in writing to insure that there is no misunderstanding by the employee as to what is expected or required.

Drug testing policies can be categorized into one of two groups: disciplinary or rehabilitative. That is, a violation of the drug use policy tends to result either in disciplinary action against the violator or a referral to an employee assistance program. Courts tend to allow an employer greater latitude in testing when the violator is referred to a program but not terminated. Some drug testing policies tend to blend both disciplinary and rehabilitative elements together. This area of the law is gray. If you feel you have been the victim of an unfair drug test, get a lawyer skilled in both labor and criminal law. Remember that drug offenses often carry very severe criminal penalties which may influence whether it is in your best interest to contest your termination or discipline. You never should put yourself in a position of admitting drug use until you have spoken with a lawyer skilled in criminal defense.

Never put yourself in a position of admitting drug use until you have spoken with a lawyer.

Invasion of the Home

Employees have won money damages after successfully suing their employers for intrusions of privacy. But the law of privacy in the work place is also gray and varies greatly from state to state. Generally, courts tend to hold that an employee has a kind of sliding scale of privacy while at work depending upon his activity and his reasonable expectations of privacy while at work. The more personal the activity (using the rest room as apposed to eating in the lunchroom) the more likely the court will declare the employer off limits. Similarly, reasonable expectations of privacy will be protected (a locked locker as opposed to a desk top).

Where the intrusions involve the worker's home, the courts are very protective. For example, in *Love v. Southern Bell Telephone and Telegraph*, 263 So.2nd 460 (La. App. 1972), the boss went to a worker's home who had called in sick. The boss thought the worker lied about being sick. He found him passed out and surrounded by whiskey bottles and beer cans in his home. After he was fired, the employee successfully sued, on grounds his privacy had been violated. The court rejected the employer's claim that the intrusion into the worker's home was motivated simply by the employer's interest concern for the worker's health.

Violations of privacy by an employer, when they occur at the worker's home, constitute much better grounds for claims against the employer than if the invasions occur at the place of work.

Confidential Information

Courts are protective of the worker's privacy over confidential and private information.

Another area where the courts are protective of the worker's privacy is over confidential and private information. If an employer discloses private information about an employee without his consent, there may be liability. Cases have held such private information to include facts about an employee's infection with the HIV virus, psychiatric treatment, cosmetic surgeries or criminal arrests without convictions. It is easy to understand protection of private information. Such facts, when not used judiciously, could subject the worker to scorn or ridicule, or otherwise affect his ability to carry on the affairs of daily life.

The general rule is that the courts will be very protective of a worker's right to be free from an employer's intrusion where the intrusion violates the sanctity of the worker's home, or involves private and embarrassing information about the employee.

The courts will be less protective where the employee is at work, although some areas where the employee has a reasonable expectation of privacy are probably not searchable by the employer unless there is consent, a policy acknowledged by the employer to the contrary or an emergency. The courts are not likely to find any right to privacy at all in unlocked desks, or public and common areas of the work place.

Criminal Record

Employees who are disciplined or terminated based on criminal conduct *outside the work place* have successfully sued employers for money damages and reinstatement. For example, in one case an arrest and conviction for marijuana use which occurred outside the employer's place of business and was the sole basis for termination, was held to be improper. Similarly, in California, the California Labor Code specifically forbids an employer from taking any action against an employee because of a criminal arrest (as opposed to an arrest followed by a *conviction*).

A minority member may have a discrimination action against an employer who refuses to hire him simply because he has been arrested. The theory is that since it has been specifically recognized that minority members are arrested in greater proportion than the general population, an employer who refuses to hire for that reason alone is making a decision which has a *disparate impact* type discrimination. This is suggested by a number of successful cases and the EEOC Compliance Manual Section N:6005 and EEOC Notice No. N-15-061. For more infor-

The courts are not likely to find any right to privacy in public and common areas of the work place.

mation about the *disparate impact* theory of discrimination under Title VII, see the discussion about the same on page 32.

Bankruptcy and Debt

If a worker who is otherwise adequately performing his employment duties files for bankruptcy protection, an employer cannot discipline or terminate him *solely* on the basis of the worker's bankruptcy. This is because the federal Bankruptcy Act specifically forbids such action. *See* 11 U.S.C. Section 525(b).

Similarly, the federal Consumer Credit Protection Act, 15 U.S.C. Section 1671, also forbids employers from taking action against an employee based on garnishment or attachment arising out of a judgment in favor of a creditor against the employee.

An employer cannot fire you for having a bankruptcy or judgment lodged against you.

The law is clear: an employer cannot fire you for having a bankruptcy or judgment lodged against you. However, if your performance at work suffers from financial problems, this is another story. So long as there is some record of poor performance, the employer can terminate after the employee files for bankruptcy or becomes a judgment debtor.

Lie Detector Use

In 1988, Congress passed a law which almost completely banned the use of lie detectors or polygraphs as a pre-employment screening tool used by private employers. The Employee Polygraph Protection Act, 20 U.S.C. Section 2001, also bans the use of polygraphs by employers to test current employees.

Under the Act, only applicants for positions involving access to controlled substances (drugs) or security may be tested by use of a polygraph. For example, job applicants for positions with armored car, security alarm and security guard firms can be tested by use of the polygraph. There are certain restrictions which apply to this testing, however: even where polygraph testing is permitted, the test results may not be the sole basis upon which employment is denied or terminated. Also, older employees may be tested due to an exception from the general ban against lie detector testing, but they are entitled to numerous protections concerning how the test is conducted.

Polygraph test results may not be the sole basis upon which employment is denied or terminated.

The Act generally *prohibits* the use of lie detectors for current employees, *except* that polygraph testing is permitted of certain employees as a part of an ongoing investigation concerning a financial loss to the company when one of the following conditions applies:

- the employee to be tested had access to the property that is the subject of the investigation;

- the employer has a reasonable suspicion that the employee was involved in the activity under investigation;

- the employer prepares a statement which points out the specific financial loss or injury, the employee's access, and the reason for the employer's reasonable suspicion that the employee was involved in the incident.

You should also know that the act does not remove or weaken any protections against lie detector testing which may be present because of any state or local law or any labor agreement. These protections, if any, exist side by side with the federal law. The Act is enforced by the Department of Labor. Relief in the courts is also available against employers who fail to follow the Act. You may file a complaint with the local office of the Wage and Hour Division of the United States Department of Labor.

Violations of the Act are punishable by a fine of up to $10,000. The court may also order that the employer reinstate or promote you and pay you for back wages.

Additional information is available through:

Wage and Hour Division
Employment Standards Administration
Department of Labor
200 Constitution Ave., NW, Room S-3502
Washington, DC 20210
(202) 523-8305

AIDS in the Workplace

AIDS is not transmitted by typical work place contact such as sharing a work station.

As the disease of Acquired Immune Deficiency Syndrome (AIDS) expands and more persons are diagnosed as having AIDS or being HIV positive, interesting issues arise in the context of employment law. The medical establishment has indicated that the disease is only transmitted by sexual contact or blood exchange, and not by other kinds of typical work place contact such as shaking hands, sharing a work station or sharing other facilities with an infected person.

There are a number of laws which protect employees with AIDS or who test HIV positive. Many people, including employers, discriminate against such persons, despite the fact it is medically understood that the disease cannot be transmitted by regular work contact.

While no AIDS specific legislation has been passed, in 1987 the United States Supreme Court held that an individual who had an infectious disease (in this case tuberculosis) was considered a "handicapped individual" under the Federal Rehabilitation Act of 1973. If you wish to read the case, it is called *School Board of Nassau County v. Arline.* You may have to visit a law library to find it. Ask the law librarian for 480 U.S. 273.

One year after this decision, the 9th Circuit Court of Appeals held that a person with AIDS was also considered a "handicapped individual." *Chalk v. United States District Court*, 840 F.2d 701 (9th Cir. 1988).

In the *Chalk* case, the plaintiff was a teacher for hearing impaired children who was diagnosed as having AIDS. When it was learned that he had the disease, the state removed him from classroom duties and assigned him to desk work. The teacher sued and the lower court denied him relief. The 9th Circuit (the appeals court) agreed with Chalk and held that casual contact in performing his teaching duties presented no significant risk to others. The 9th Circuit also noted that Chalk was handicapped but he was also *otherwise qualified* to carry out his duties as a teacher.

There are a number of laws which protect employees with AIDS or who test HIV positive.

Assuming that one with AIDS or who tests HIV positive is a qualified handicapped individual, the Rehabilitation Act of 1973, 20 U.S.C. Section 701, prevents discrimination of any kind. If persons with AIDS or HIV are qualified handicapped individuals, then companies must make reasonable accommodations for such individuals. This Act is important because it covers not only employees with actual handicaps, but also those with a *perceived handicap*. In March, 1988, Congress amended the Rehabilitation Act's definition of *handicap* stating that the Act does not cover persons with contagious diseases or infection, *if because of the disease or infection* the person constitutes a direct threat to the health or safety of others or is unable to perform his or her job. The Office of Federal Contract Compliance Programs (OFCCP) enforces this provision. Keep in mind that a covered employee who has a grievance must file a charge with OFCCP within 180 days of the alleged act of discrimination.

The ADA requires employers to make reasonable accomodations to workers disabled because of AIDS.

As was discussed previously, the ADA prohibits an employer from discriminating against a qualified individual with a disability because of that disability. The ADA also requires that employers make reasonable accommodations to qualified disabled employees. This includes workers disabled because of AIDS or HIV.

The ADA covers both employees with AIDS and those who test positive for HIV. It applies the rules of reasonable accommodation to people with AIDS. Also, discrimination against those with AIDS is forbidden by Title VII of the Civil Rights Act of 1964, 42 U.S.C. Section 2000(e)(5)(e). Remember that the law requires that any complaints be filed within 180 days of the act of discrimination.

Finally, your state constitution or state civil rights acts may prohibit discrimination in employment on the basis of race, color, religion, sex, age, handicap or national origin, or other basis. So it is possible that under your state law, AIDS or HIV positive would be considered a handicap and would constitute grounds for filing a complaint against an employer who discriminated against an employee based on such a condition.

This is an area of the law where you need competent legal help. In addition to complaints that you may have which should be forwarded to the OFCCP or EEOC, you probably have certain common law causes of action, that is, grounds for suit in your state court or federal district court based on invasion of privacy, breach of contract, defamation, intentional infliction of emotional distress and wrongful discharge.

For more information, contact:

Affirmative Action of Handicapped Persons
Office of Federal Compliance Programs
Employment Standards Administration
Department of Labor
200 Constitution Ave., NW, Room C-3325
Washington, DC 20210
(202) 523-9475

Credit and Background Checks

So long as an employer has a legitimate business need regarding your bill paying habits, he can obtain your records.

So long as an employer has a *legitimate business need* for information regarding your bill paying habits, the employer can obtain your records from a credit reporting service. The employer is not required to tell you he is accessing your files, nor is the credit reporting service required to advise you that someone has asked to look up your credit and that they have responded accordingly.

However, the Fair Credit Reporting Act of 1970 penalizes those who obtain information from a credit service without a *legitimate business need*. Since this is a very elastic standard, and potential employers probably do have a legitimate need to know how you have handled your affairs in that this arguably reflects on how you might handle your responsibilities as an employee, most courts will probably consider it appropriate that an employer obtain credit information. However, in order to make sure that your credit history is accurate, you should obtain your own credit report and make any appropriate corrections at least once per year.

You should obtain your own credit report and make any appropriate corrections at least once per year.

Employer Searches and Surveillance

As I said in the section discussing drug testing, non-governmental employers are generally free to invade your privacy during working hours and while you are on the premises of the employer in order to reasonably protect or further the interest of the business. I also said that although there is no constitutional protection against unreasonable searches and seizures by non-governmental employers, there is a right of privacy at the work place.

Employers are always subject to the common law of negligence, fraud, conversion, and trespass, which apply to everyone. In addition, several states, including Connecticut, Georgia, Ohio, Virginia and Wisconsin have laws which specifically ban certain kinds of surveillance and searches of employees.

Generally, an employer cannot invade your privacy by:

- pretending to get information for a legitimate purpose but using it for another purpose which is outlawed by law;

- lying to you about what the information he has requested from you is going to be used for;

- obtaining information about or from you where the employer has no reasonable business purpose in obtaining this information or material.

I recommend that you obtain your personnel file anytime you feel that your privacy has been invaded by your employer. Personnel files are a rich source of information about what the employer knows about you or your work habits.

You should obtain your personnel file anytime you feel your privacy has been invaded by your employer.

Seventeen states allow an employee to obtain or review his personnel file without filing a lawsuit. They are: Alaska, Arkansas, California, Connecticut, Delaware, Illinois, Maine, Massachusetts, Michigan, Minnesota, Nevada, New Hampshire, Oregon, Pennsylvania, Rhode Island, Washington and Wisconsin. If you live in one of these states, go to your local library for help in finding the details of the law and complying with the appropriate procedure, or hire a lawyer. You may be able to recover your attorney's fees if you sue and win. The lawyer will know how likely you are to win and what the chances are of getting your attorney's fees paid.

In all other states you will have to sue your employer to get your employment records if he will not give them to you voluntarily. This is usually done by filing a lawsuit and then making a formal request for *disclosure* or *discovery* in accordance with your state's court rules of civil procedure. You may be in for a long hard battle with your employer's law firm over these records. I strongly urge you to obtain competent counsel before filing suit. It is foolhardy to institute a suit against an employer, without competent legal counsel.

CHAPTER THIRTEEN
PROTECTING YOUR IDEAS, INVENTIONS AND THE RIGHT TO WORK WHERE YOU CHOOSE

"For Hire" Employees

Whether you are a composer, scientist, writer, or otherwise involved in creating intellectual property, if you are an employee, as opposed to an independent contractor (see Chapter 3, page 10) the general rule is that when you develop an idea which has a unique application or is otherwise valuable, your employer owns the right to that idea. In other words, the employer, and not you, will be entitled to all the future royalties and profit from this intellectual property.

However, be sure to show any employment contract that you have to a competent attorney to determine your contractual rights in this area. If there is no contract then you are a *"for hire"* employee and as such you are not entitled to share in future royalties or income derived from your creation, work or invention. If you are about to take a job in which you will be creating or inventing, get a patent or copyright lawyer to help you negotiate rights to royalties. You'll be sorry if you don't!

> *"For hire" employees are not entitled to share in royalties or income derived from their inventions.*

Trade Secrets

Every employer has the right to protect the trade secrets of his business. Trade secrets include customer names, addresses, key contracts, pricing information, and other technical or valuable information which is critical to the successful operation of the business. You can be sued by your employer for divulging these secrets, whether you have an employment contract or not. If you change employers, be very careful that you do not divulge critical information, since you can be held financially responsible for all the damages caused by your disclosure. Again, it is always wise to hire a lawyer to negotiate and draft an employment contract which minimizes the adverse consequences to you for divulging trade secrets (such as the use of a minimal limited damages clause) or overall exposure for secrets not known (such as creating an addendum to the employment contract identifying each and every secret involved in your employment).

Covenants Not to Compete

It is the burden of the employer to show that the covenant not to compete has been breached by the employee.

A covenant not to compete is a clause in an employment contract, or a separate agreement between an employee and employer in which the employee promises that for a certain period of time, the employee will not engage in any competitive enterprise within a certain geographic area. The law in all states disfavors such covenants. The policy behind the law is to encourage the free flow of commerce and to allow people the opportunity to work in whatever capacity they feel interests them. However, it is also the policy of the law to enforce contracts. It is the burden of the employer to show that the covenant not to compete has been breached by some activity of the former employee.

Generally, covenants will not be enforced where the time limitation is unreasonable (usually greater than one year) or the geographical area is too large (for example, an entire city, state or region). However, this depends on the type of job you had, the employer's industry or business and nature of the competition. The law governing covenants not to compete is established according to the court decisions and statutes of your state.

There are several factors which the courts tend to evaluate in enforcing a covenant not to compete. Remember that the key concept is what is reasonable under the circumstances. We start with the idea that a covenant is a valid agreement (there has been a meeting of the minds between the parties and some consideration given) which the court will enforce provided the following four conditions are met:

The key concept in a covenant not to compete is "what is reasonable under the circumstances."

1. The covenant is not overly restrictive of the right of the employee to find new work;

2. The covenant does not interfere with any announced public policy;

3. The covenant is reasonable and necessary for the protection of the employer's business;

4. The covenant is in writing and is part of an agreement supported by adequate consideration and is incidental to an otherwise legally enforceable contract.

It is strongly recommended that you obtain competent counsel in this area. Although the rules are relatively easy to understand, there is no specific, precise number of years or an exact amount of territory that a covenant may concern before it is declared invalid. And since every case is different, you need a lawyer's experience to help you predict what a judge or jury will decide about the covenant you are trying to avoid.

CHAPTER FOURTEEN
THE FAMILY AND MEDICAL LEAVE ACT OF 1993

In what promises to be only the beginning of a wave of federal employment law changes, President Clinton signed the Family & Medical Leave Act of 1993 (FMLA) into law on February 5, 1993. Generally, this law only applies to employers which have 50 or more employees to be covered. Thus, 95% of all businesses—those employing fewer than 50 employees—are not covered by the new law.

Family leave is not new. In 1978, the Federal Pregnancy Discrimination Act required employers to allow workers to take time off to care for newborns. A number of states already had some form of unpaid family and medical leave, including California, Minnesota, Maine, Connecticut, New Jersey, Rhode Island, Washington, Oregon, Wisconsin and the District of Columbia. Your state law may provide similar protection.

For an employee working for a covered employer to be eligible to invoke rights under FMLA law, he must have been employed for at least one year and have provided at least 1,250 hours of service during the 12 months before leave is requested.

To invoke rights under FMLA law, you must have been employed for at least one year.

Eligible employees are entitled to 12 unpaid work weeks for any one of the following three reasons during any 12-month period: 1) birth or placement for adoption or foster care of a child; 2) serious health condition of a spouse, son, daughter, or parent; or, 3) the employee's own serious health condition. An employee's right to leave for the birth or adoption of a child ends 12 months after the child's birth or placement with the employee.

Other than leave for birth or adoption, the leave must meet the standard of being for a *serious health condition*. A *serious health condition* is a physical or mental condition or illness that involves in-patient care or continuing treatment by a health care provider. Where the employee seeks leave for his own *serious health condition*, a qualifying condition is that the employee is unable to perform the functions of the job. Employers can require employees to use accrued paid leave—for example, vacation, personal or sick leave—as part of the 12-week period.

FMLA permits the employer to require an eligible employee to provide a doctor's certification in support of the leave request and to do so in a timely manner. The employer can also, at its expense, require that the eligible employee obtain a second opinion. In the event of a conflict in the medical opinions, the Act provides for a third opinion rendered by a health care provider designated jointly by the employer and employee. This opinion shall be final and binding and is to be paid for by the employer. Further recertification of the employee's need for leave may be required by the employer on a *reasonable* basis.

Employees on leave are entitled to have their health care coverage continued.

Employees on leave are entitled to have their health care coverage continued at the level and under the conditions such coverage would have been provided if the employee had continued in active employment during the period of the leave. Under certain circumstances, where the employee does not return from leave, the employer may recover from the employee health insurance premiums paid for maintaining coverage.

FMLA also states that returning employees must be returned to their position or an equivalent position with equivalent employment benefits and pay. But, an employee is not entitled to accrue benefits or seniority during that leave period. The employer may exempt the highest paid 10% of its work force, if denying such employee's leave is necessary to prevent serious economic harm to the operations of the employer.

FMLA requires the employee to provide 30 days advance notice if the necessity for the leave is foreseeable based on an expected birth or adoption or a planned medical treatment stemming from a serious medical condition. If the date of the birth, adoption placement, or planned medical treatment requires leave to begin in less than 30 days, the employee must provide such notice as is practicable. Employees are also required to make a reasonable effort to schedule treatments for serious health conditions so as not to unnecessarily disrupt the operations of the employer.

Interestingly, FMLA permits leave to be taken on a piecemeal or staggered basis under certain circumstances. The Act provides that *intermittent* or *leave on a reduced leave schedule* may be taken to care for a newborn or newly-adopted child so long as the employer consents to this arrangement. Leave for serious health conditions may also be taken on a piecemeal basis, even in the absence of employer consent, if such intermittent leave is medically necessary.

Interestingly, FMLA permits leave to be taken on a piecemeal basis under certain circumstances.

The Act further declares that if such leave for a serious health condition is foreseeable based on planned medical treatment, the employer is permitted to temporarily transfer the employee to an alternative position. This alternative position, for which the employee is qualified, must have equivalent pay and benefits and serve to better accommodate periodic periods of leave than the employee's regular position. Other provisions of the FMLA include:

If leave for a health condition is foreseeable, the employer can transfer you to an alternative position.

- Spouses employed by the same employer are subject to a restriction. Their total leave in any 12-month period may be limited to 12 weeks when the leave is taken for the birth or adoption of a child or to care for a sick parent;

- Regulations will be issued by the Department of Labor within 120 days from the passage of this law. Enforcement will be patterned after the Fair Labor Standard Act;

- It is unlawful to interfere with the exercise of rights under the Act. It is further unlawful to discriminate against any individual complaining about violations of the Act;

- The effective date of the Act is 6 months from February 5, 1993, the date of its enactment. But, where a collective bargaining agreement is applicable, the Act shall take effect upon the termination of the agreement, but in no event later than 12 months from the date of the enactment of the law.

Finally, the FMLA states that employers who violate worker's rights are liable to the employee for monetary damages and reinstatement or promotion, if applicable. Any lawsuit must be filed within two years of the last event constituting the violation, or within three years if the violation is willful. If you sue, you may file in either state or federal court.

CONCLUSION

Employment law is complex and confusing! There is a superbowl sized container of government agencies, federal laws and state statutes together with a non-stop flow of state and federal court decisions interpreting and reinterpreting the whole mess, making it tough sledding for lawyers. Lay folks have poor odds trying to figure things out on their own. This a shame because the law is all of ours. It is not just for lawyers. This little book at least has some telephone numbers to get you started! The alphabet agencies and the alphabet statutes are part of a well-intentioned bureaucracy that may be frustrating to deal with, but if you are patient and able to understand the agency system and the concept behind the law, you can figure it out.

You bought this book either because 1) you are interested in knowing your rights or 2) you've got a problem you need help in solving. For folks in the former category, I thank you and encourage you to learn all you can about our clunky but magnificent system which I'm proud, as an American lawyer, to work with. For those in the latter group, I thank you for trusting me to help you with your problems and I truly hope that my book helps you understand your situation better so you'll have some idea of what you can and cannot do. Good luck!

Richard L. Strohm, Esq.
7373 N. Scottsdale Road, Suite 130-C
Scottsdale, Arizona 85253
(602) 951-2653
December, 1993

APPENDIX

Employment Information Form

U.S. Department of Labor
Employment Standards Administration
Wage and Hour Division

This report is authorized by Section 11 of the Fair Labor Standards Act. While you are not required to respond, submission of this information is necessary for the Division to schedule any compliance action. Your identity will be kept confidential to the maximum extent possible under existing law.

OMB No. 1215-0001
Expires: 09-30-92

1. Person Submitting Information

A. Name (Print first name, middle initial, and last name)

Mr.

Miss

Mrs.

Ms.

B. Date

C. Telephone number:
(Or No. where you can be reached)

D. Address: (Number, Street, Apt. No.)

(City, County, State, ZIP Code)

E. Check one of these boxes

☐ Present employee of establishment   ☐ Former employee of establishment   ☐ Other

(Specify: relative, union, etc)

2. Establishment Information

A. Name of establishment

B. Telephone Number

C. Address of establishment: (Number, Street)

(City, County, State, ZIP Code)

D. Estimate number of employees

E. Does the firm have branches?   ☐ Yes   ☐ No   ☐ Don't know

If "Yes", name one or two locations:

F. Nature of establishment's business: (For example: school, farm, hospital, hotel, restaurant, shoe store, wholesale drugs, manufactures stoves, coal mine, construction, trucking, etc.)

G. If the establishment has a Federal Government or federally assisted contract, check the appropriate box(es).

☐ Furnishes goods   ☐ Furnishes services   ☐ Performs construction

H. Does establishment ship goods to or receive goods from other States?

☐ Yes   ☐ No   ☐ Don't know

3. Employment Information (Complete A, B, C, D, E, & F if present or former employee of establishment; otherwise complete F only)

A. Period employed (month, year)

From:

To:
(If still there, state present)

B. Date of birth if under 19

Month _____ Day _____ Year _____

C. Give your job title and describe briefly the kind of work you do

(Continue on other side)

Form WH-3
Rev. 10/99

115

Index

119